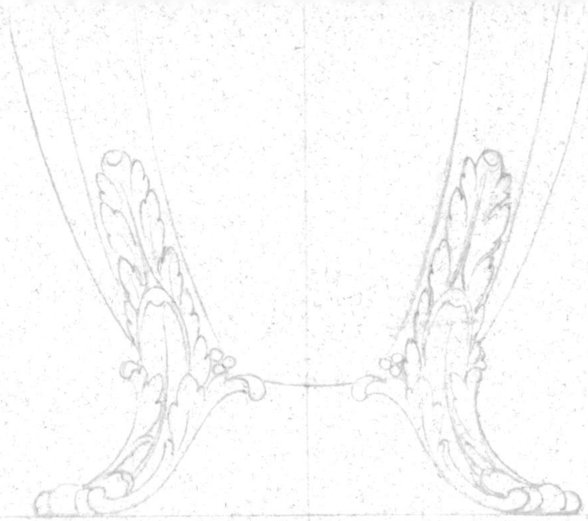

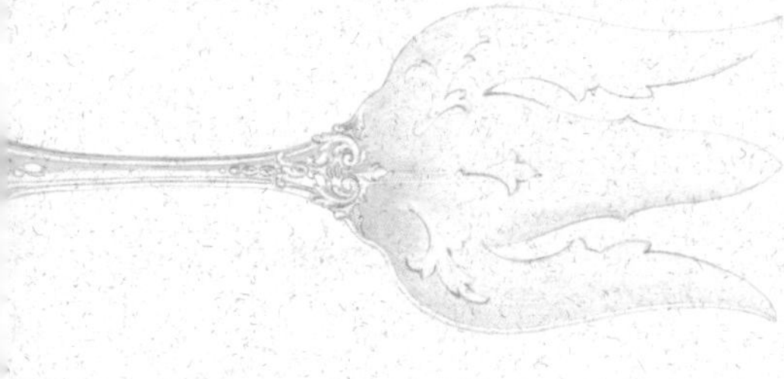

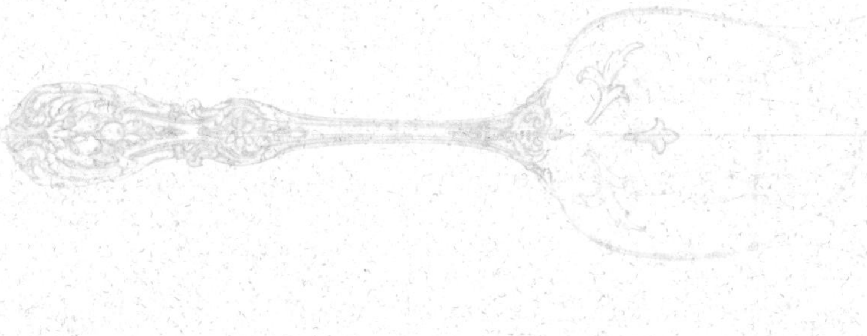

Sterling Seasons

The Reed & Barton Story

Sterling Seasons

The Reed & Barton Story

RENEE GARRELICK

Reed & Barton Corporation Taunton, Massachusetts 1998

ISBN 0-9663261-0-5

Library of Congress Catalog Card Number 98-66010

Book Design by David Ford

Frontispiece, Francis I flatware, first produced in 1908, continues to be the leading sterling pattern for Reed & Barton. 1997. Reed & Barton archives.

Sterling Seasons

is dedicated to all

who have been a part of Reed & Barton,

those within the company's employ

and those who employ its products.

CONTENTS

EMBRACING A LEGACY

THE ONE HUNDRED seventy-fifth anniversary of Reed & Barton was not the impetus for the history *Sterling Seasons: The Reed & Barton Story*; it did, however dictate its deadline. Chairman Sinclair Weeks Jr. was the driving force for a history to be written. Reed & Barton has been more than his career for the past forty years. It has been his legacy from birth, going back to his great-grandfather Henry Reed. His maternal grandfather, William Dowse, succeeded Reed as president and was followed by his father, Sinclair Weeks. Harvard University and the Harvard Business School had been attended by members of the family; and when the Harvard Business School approached the company for the inclusion of Reed & Barton in their analysis of business case studies in 1941, Sinclair Weeks readily agreed. The resulting book, *The Whitesmiths of Taunton* by George Sweet Gibb, was published in 1943 by Harvard University Press.

Sinclair Weeks Jr. had long been eager to bring the company's story up to the present and his invitation to me as a writer of New England and business history was made even more appealing by his close family connection to Reed & Barton. A visit to the company reveals that the Reed & Barton family extends beyond management to many employees and their relations who have worked for the company for generations. Such continuity of employment and length of service is rare in our mobile society, and a tour of the plant with Sinclair Weeks Jr. shows the bond of mutual affection with staff. The Reed & Barton site includes its original buildings, listed on the National Register of Historic Places, that draw one back in time to the early days of the Industrial Revolution. The company's history mirrors the evolution of this country.

A new book would be written about one of the oldest manufacturing companies in the nation and one of only two privately owned silver companies today.

In an era of acquisitions, mergers, and bankruptcies, the continuance of Reed & Barton as a family-owned company reaching one hundred seventy-five years is a significant passage to be recognized. While a milestone anniversary did not occasion the book's publication, the history written would become a natural feature of the company commemorative. As a result, the small window of time available for the project was both a stimulant and a decisive challenge.

Reed & Barton is an engaging company to get to know. From the moment one walks through the "silver doors," the intimacy of scale contributes to a personable, comfortable feeling. Reed & Barton never loses its human dimension, an atmosphere reflective of the management style that is seen throughout the operations of the company. When Reed & Barton tent sales bring the company and public together, management joins in as wait staff to assist customers in the festive chase for good buys. Here is a company easy to bond and identify with.

Director of Advertising and Sales Promotion John Ehrlich, Public Relations Manager Marci Karales, and Personnel Director Candace Lofgren provided valued assistance in assembling materials for *Sterling Seasons;* and Corporate Photographer Dan Sweeney contributed the essential visual dimension of contemporary Reed & Barton through product photographs. I have worked with copy editor Jane Benes on many projects that have benefited from her high standards and supportive enthusiasm. Reed & Barton silverware has been part of her family life since childhood, so there was special interest in getting to know the company's history. Our singular regret was that the colleges we attended during the 1960s were not part of a Reed & Barton opinion survey. We would have enjoyed offering our pattern preference, entering contests for prizes, and at the very least receiving a silver spoon to pin on our sweaters.

From the day I first met with Chairman Sinclair Weeks Jr., President Al Krebel, and Treasurer Charles Terry to discuss the book, they nurtured my sense of belonging. I felt a part of Reed & Barton as I gathered as much about the company as I could learn from its archives and through conversations with current and retired staff. Their voices tell the story; they speak for many individuals over the years, lifetimes of contribution and expressions of affection for the company. My efforts were directed not towards the pursuit of independent scholarship but towards representing these voices accurately. In doing so I could best present the Reed & Barton story and best embrace its legacy.

Renee Garrelick, Concord, Massachusetts 1998

Sterling Seasons

The Reed & Barton Story

ON THE BANKS OF THE MILL RIVER

> Here Time speaks, for everything is old. These things we see are survivors of their time reclining now to pass on through the years the record of their part in progress.
>
> –Phillip L. Sniffin, *A Century of Silversmithing, 1824–1924*

SILVERWARE ENGAGES the eye of the designer. Named the "queen of metals," silver extends beyond functional use to representations of culture and contributions to art. The luster of silver attracted the ancient alchemists who called it *luna* and gave it the crescent moon as a symbol. The whitest of all metals, with the highest optical reflectivity, silver is also extremely malleable and ductile and can be rolled and hammered into thin foil or leaf, and one ounce drawn into thousands of feet of wire.

Decorations cut in stone portraying the craft of silversmithing date back to twenty-five hundred years before the birth of Christ. Silver spoons were biblical objects; the ancient Egyptians valued silver more than gold, and silver has been used as currency from the Greeks and Romans into modern times. Silver, once crafted for the use of the church, kings, and the very wealthy, reached the workingman's table during the twentieth century.

"Every currency between the Nile and the Euphrates in ancient cultures was based on silver," relates Sinclair Weeks Jr. "Then the Greeks, many of whom had settled in Asia Minor, acquired the knowledge of silver mining. The great mines at Laurium financed the Athenian wars against the Persians. After the Romans gained control, they brought the knowledge of silver mining to Spain, by then a part of the Roman Empire. The Spaniards mined rich and extensive lodes and began a trade with India through the Red Sea in exchange for the silks, satins, and jewels of that subcontinent. The largest source of silver above ground today is still around the ankles, wrists, and necks of the women of India.

"When the New World opened up, the Spaniards took the knowledge of silver mining to Central America, and the next important developments in silver min-

Reed & Barton workers enjoy a company outing. The lives of workers revolved around the company both on and off the job during the nineteenth century. 1865. Reed & Barton archives.

The *Diamond* sterling tea set by contemporary product designer John Prip of Reed & Barton was created to complement the *Diamond* flatware pattern designed by Italian architect Gio Ponti. *Left to right*: Coffee Pot, Sugar Bowl, Cream Pitcher, Waste Bowl, Tea Pot, on Waiter. 1958. Reed & Barton archives.

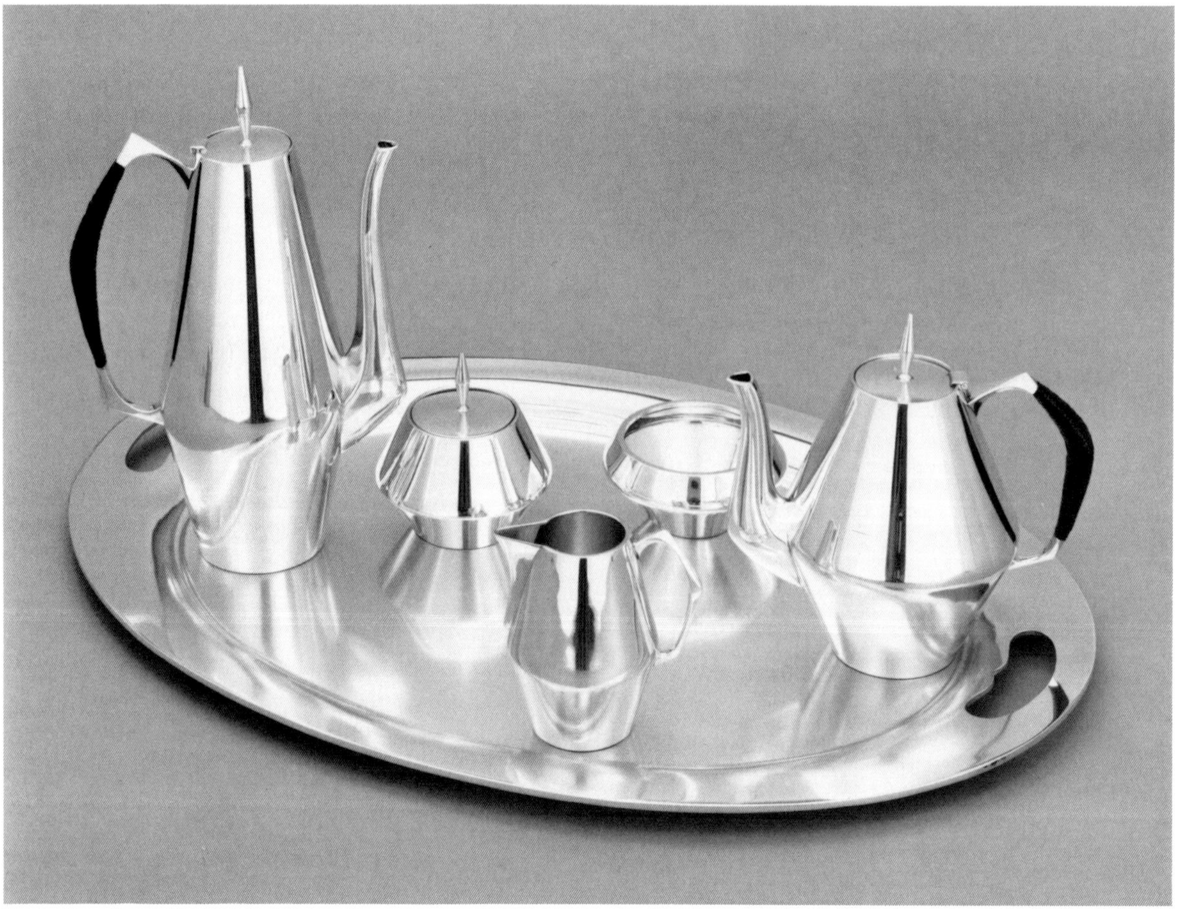

Above, King Francis silver-plated punch bowl set.

Below, Francis I sterling tea set.

ing were the mines in Central and South America," relates Weeks. "Then in our own country came the large Comstock Lode strike in Nevada which had a lot to do with getting our company and competitors into the sterling business. Today the four major producers of silver in order of importance are Mexico, Canada, then the United States and Peru exchanging third and fourth position. The purest seams of silver were found near the surface, enabling nineteenth-century miners to dig silver out easily, but one hundred years later the amount of metal in each ton of ore diminished as mines were dug deeper. Silver is now considered a bonus, when miners retrieve base metals of copper, lead, and zinc, which when smelted leave small fractions of silver."

England was a world leader for fine silver and workmanship, and the tradition inevitably spread to its American colony. Much of the silverware from the early-eighteenth-century Queen Anne period was made by French Huguenot silversmiths who fled to England, and the work of Paul DeLamerie was the best known, relates Weeks. Some came to this country, one of whom was Adolphus Rivoire, who changed his name to Revere and became father to the famous silversmith and patriot Paul Revere.

Most flatware for general use was found only in prosperous homes. In the days of Queen Elizabeth I, for example, only royalty used forks. Most of her subjects carried a short, broad-bladed knife that they kept in their belts, and spoons were made of wood or horn. President John Adams and his wife Abigail reportedly became quite a topic of conversation by using forks they had brought back from France. In colonial days a silver coffee pot was made from start to finish by just one man, while today it may require as many as sixty operations and the work of many to assure the consumer uniformity of size, shape, weight, detail, and quality. One Reed & Barton *Francis I* sterling fork requires twenty-seven separate operations.

The founders of Reed & Barton were craftsmen; Henry Reed, a spinner, and Charles Barton, a solderer, started at the bench and continued to do so as managers. Whether as a spinner or as president of Reed & Barton, Henry Reed had an intense interest in quality. When his nephew Nat Cushman in 1877 asked his uncle if he might have a slightly dented water pitcher as a "second," Reed's response was to smash the pitcher to the floor saying, "Young man, we don't make seconds around here." *The Whitesmiths of Taunton* observed that "Reed & Barton owes its birth and continued existence to the demands of the American people for something finer than their fathers had possessed."

The entrance silver doors of Reed & Barton.

Well into the mid twentieth century Taunton, Massachusetts, was called Silver City for this once prospering industry. The Taunton Silver Company, Taunton Britannia Company, Bennett Silver Company, Cohannet Silver Company, F. B. Rogers Silver Company, H. O. Rogers Silver Company, Poole Silver Company, and the National Silver Company have closed their doors and only Reed & Barton remains.

Because of its significance as the oldest industry in Taunton operating continuously on the same site and as one of the oldest silver companies in the nation, the Reed & Barton complex of buildings received nomination to the National Register of Historic Places. At the ceremony held 27 June 1986 in recognition, local and state officials spoke of the contribution of Taunton workers to a company known internationally for the quality of its products. "Over the years the cream of the crop of the people of the City of Taunton have worked here, and they have done a magnificent job in producing a product that's known all over the world."

SCIENTIFIC AMERICAN

[Entered at the Post Office of New York, N. Y., as Second Class Matter.]

A WEEKLY JOURNAL OF PRACTICAL INFORMATION, ART, SCIENCE, MECHANICS, CHEMISTRY, AND MANUFACTURES.

Vol. XLI.—No. 19. [NEW SERIES.] | NEW YORK, NOVEMBER 8, 1879. | [$3.20 per Annum. [POSTAGE PREPAID.]

JUST PUTTING ONE DOLLAR ON TOP OF ANOTHER

THE NEWLY formed nation that had fought for its political independence was still dependent upon Europe for a large part of its manufactured goods. The founders of Reed & Barton struggled for industrial independence fifty years later. They believed that Americans could make goods for their own market as well or better than workers abroad. They strove to earn that right, facing foreign competition and the need for public acceptance.

Generally, the early silversmiths combined their craft with another trade. Paul Revere was also a bronze foundryman and copperplate engraver, while others were clock and watchmakers, blacksmiths, or jewelry makers. The Babbitt family were gadget makers in Taunton, and Isaac Babbitt opened his jewelry store on Merchants' Row in 1822 with a small shed as a workshop at the rear. The village jeweler manufactured many of the products that he sold and serviced the minor mechanical needs of the community.

Isaac Babbitt, aware that people were asking for the shiny new Britannia metal tableware from English factories, became interested in its property, an alloy of tin that was 92 percent tin, 6 percent antimony, and 2 percent copper. It was similar to pewter but with a sheen almost that of silver. Production costs were lower, and a much less expensive product could be marketed to the general public for use as durable metal table utensils. In 1769 James Vickers was the first to begin making Britannia ware, or white metal, in Sheffield, England; and in 1804 James Dickson in Sheffield established the leading producing factory. From 1816 large quantities of Britannia ware were imported to America, where several attempts were made to reproduce them.

Scenes from the Reed & Barton factory were featured on the cover of the 8 November 1879 issue of *Scientific American.*

Babbitt and his friend William Porter, familiar with the metal used at his fa-

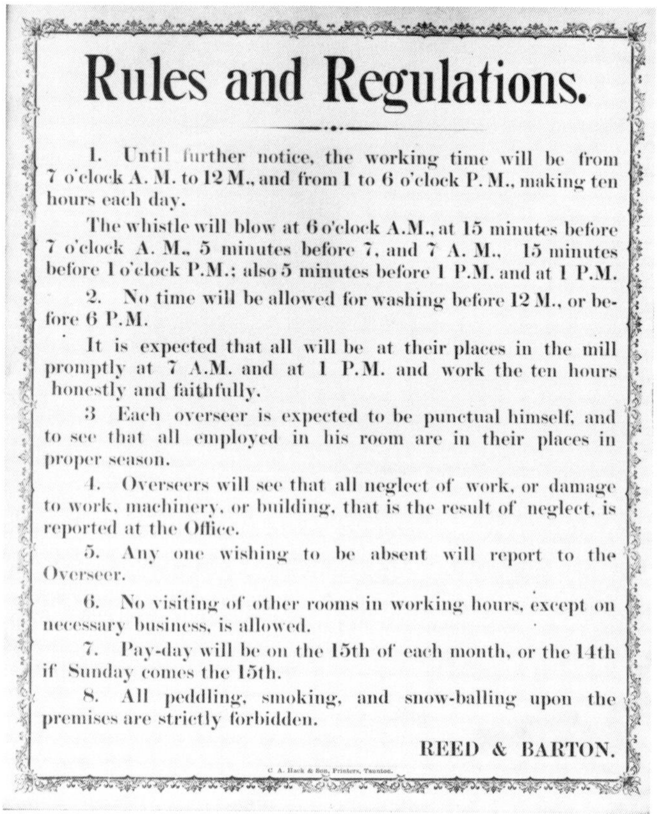

Rules and Regulations.

1. Until further notice, the working time will be from 7 o'clock A. M. to 12 M., and from 1 to 6 o'clock P. M., making ten hours each day.

The whistle will blow at 6 o'clock A.M., at 15 minutes before 7 o'clock A. M., 5 minutes before 7, and 7 A. M., 15 minutes before 1 o'clock P.M.; also 5 minutes before 1 P.M. and at 1 P.M.

2. No time will be allowed for washing before 12 M., or before 6 P.M.

It is expected that all will be at their places in the mill promptly at 7 A.M. and at 1 P.M. and work the ten hours honestly and faithfully.

3 Each overseer is expected to be punctual himself, and to see that all employed in his room are in their places in proper season.

4. Overseers will see that all neglect of work, or damage to work, machinery, or building, that is the result of neglect, is reported at the Office.

5. Any one wishing to be absent will report to the Overseer.

6. No visiting of other rooms in working hours, except on necessary business, is allowed.

7. Pay-day will be on the 15th of each month, or the 14th if Sunday comes the 15th.

8. All peddling, smoking, and snow-balling upon the premises are strictly forbidden.

REED & BARTON.

C. A. Hack & Son, Printers, Taunton.

Above, The rules of the house. Posted factory rules and regulations. 1880. Reed & Barton archives.

Right, Silverplated engraved tea set. 1885 Catalogue. Reed & Barton archives.

Isaac Babbitt, 1799–1862. Taunton jeweler, who developed an alloy for the first Britannia ware in America. Reed & Barton archives.

Charles E. Barton, 1812–1867. A solderer and close-working partner with Henry Reed for thirty-two years. Reed & Barton archives.

Henry Gooding Reed, 1810–1901. A spinner, whose leadership as president governed Reed & Barton's high standards for quality craftsmanship. Reed & Barton archives.

ther's pewter button shop, experimented with various combinations and melts of antimony, copper, tin, lead, and zinc, persisting in the idea that Britannia ware could be manufactured in Taunton. Early in May 1824 the experiments and search for the right alloy of Britannia metal proved successful. As recorded by Porter's son Edmund, Babbitt said, "Well, Porter, I believe I have got it at last, and if you will help turn the rolls we will see if it will prove good metal." The first sheet of Britannia ware was before them.

Another jeweler William Crossman was interested in Babbitt's discovery and they formed the partnership Babbitt & Crossman, using the rear of the Merchants' Row jewelry store to manufacture their first Britannia products, and soon moved to larger rented quarters on Spring Street. Their early products included Britannia inkstands, shaving boxes, looking glass frames, and cups.

Taunton was a good place for manufacturing. Mercantile interests developed early in the town's history, accessible from the coast entirely by water routes, providing economical means of importing bulky raw material and shipping finished products to markets along the Atlantic seaboard. There was an abundance of bog iron, waterpower, and wood, attractive to manufacturing interests. Some said Taunton, with a population then of 4,500, was too busy and prosperous to be attractive, and quiet colonial charm never languished between the Mill and Taunton Rivers. In 1824 a stage line ran regularly from Taunton to Boston, while boat and wagon communication was maintained with Providence, Newport, and New Bedford, all prominent shipping centers.

The Reed & Barton story began with an experiment to manufacture Britannia and developed through its replacement by plated silverware and the ascendancy of sterling silver following the Civil War. The company underwent a series of ownerships as Babbitt & Crossman, 7 May 1824; Babbitt, Crossman & Company, December 1827; Crossman, West & Leonard, 19 February 1829; Taunton Britannia Manufacturing Co., 18 August 1830; Leonard, Reed & Barton, 20 February 1837; and as Reed & Barton, established 26 August 1840.

The growing enterprise was in search of better facilities and sufficient waterpower for its needs. In 1826 the new two-story brick shop opened on Lafayette Street, now School Street, opposite the Central Fire Station. At the School Street location a James rotary engine, the first steam power in Taunton, was installed; and in 1827 the company started the manufacture of Britannia tea ware. A teapot featured in the jewelry store window as the first of its kind made in America created much interest, and "eighteen sets were immediately ordered."

Britannia metal cider pitcher, circa 1830–1840, designed and produced by Roswell Gleason, who was active as a pewterer from 1821 to 1871. Gleason's business was acquired by Reed & Barton and his tools used to reproduce the pitcher for a commission by Marshall Field department store in 1968 commemorating the 150th anniversary of Illinois joining the union. Reed & Barton collection.

Left, Reed & Barton Britannia Tea Set No. 1507, made in the early 1840s and one of the first wares to bear the Reed & Barton mark. Collection of Robert H. Bury. (Robert H. Bury grew up in one of the Reed & Barton company homes. His father, Matt Bury, became vice president of sales; his mother, Lena Lamoureux, was secretary to President Arthur Ashworth, and his grandfather Joseph Lamoureux was foreman of the repair department. Bury is a collector of early American Britannia ware, with a special proclivity for those pieces manufactured by Reed & Barton.)

Right, Reed & Barton silverplated candelabrum, five light #800. Manufactured in the early 1900s, revived in the 1950s. Collection of Robert H. Bury.

Right, Britannia teapot bearing Leonard Reed & Barton name, circa 1837–40. Reed & Barton collection.

Far right, Pewter water pitcher, circa 1840. Reed & Barton collection.

Reed & Barton factory and horse-drawn wagons. Circa 1870. Reed & Barton archives.

William Allan West owned a dry goods shop next to Babbitt's and in December 1827 invested in the new enterprise, and the partnership of Babbitt, Crossman & Company was formed. They were youthful entrepreneurs with Babbitt age twenty-eight, Crossman age thirty-three, and West age twenty-six. In February 1829 Babbitt sold his interest in the partnership to Zephaniah Leonard from a prominent Taunton family, and the new partnership of Crossman, West & Leonard was established. Babbitt remained as plant superintendent of the operation, Porter as foreman, and Leonard as the outside investor. By the fall of 1829 there were twenty-two employees, including Charles Barton who came in 1827 at age nineteen and Henry Reed who arrived in 1828 at age eighteen.

More capital was needed and the partnership ended on 18 August 1830 with the parties forming a new joint stock company, called the Taunton Britannia Manufacturing Company, which shortly after moved to the present site on the Mill River in the area of Taunton then called Hopewell and later Whittenton. The Hopewell site on the Mill River offered excellent waterpower on a small scale. The new structure made of brick, one hundred feet long, forty feet wide, and three stories high, was the first of several buildings and still stands on West Britannia Street.

The number of employees grew to fifty-five by May 1832. At this time West and Leonard left the company, each selling his interest to Leonard's son Horatio. The early 1830s proved to be a difficult economic climate for the struggling company. Items were sold largely on consignment, and credit to finance production was not easy to obtain. The company failed in November 1834, and there was no production during the winter of 1834 or in 1835. It was at this point that Henry Reed and Charles Barton were approached by sales agent Benjamin Pratt with the idea that they assume control over the business and rent the shop from Horatio Leonard. With equipment otherwise idle it was worth a try for all parties. On 1 April 1835 the Taunton Britannia Manufacturing Company began with new management and eleven employees. Horatio Leonard transferred his interest to his son Gustavus in the operating partnership of Leonard, Reed & Barton. The depression of 1837 had reduced the number of employees to five before the company was able to turn around. On 26 August 1840 Reed & Barton purchased Leonard's interest in the tools and stock available, and the company of Reed & Barton began with Gustavus Leonard continuing to work for the company as salesman and treasurer. The Leonard, Reed & Barton mark continued to be used until 1847 when the estate of Gustavus Leonard was settled following his unexpected death in 1845.

When Henry Reed walked into the Lafayette Street shop on a May morning in 1828, William Crossman introduced him to foreman William Porter. “Here, Porter, is a boy that wants to learn a trade; you set him to work and see what he will amount to.” Henry Reed began work as an apprentice spinner under the guidance of William Crossman, then a partner of Isaac Babbitt, who hired him at forty-two cents a day. In 1834 Crossman secured a patent on a development of the spinning process that could turn out a complete form in one operation and represented a significant technological development both for the company and the industry.

Most trade was on credit, from one to nine months, and customers’ notes or drafts were usually discounted 10 percent. In the 1830s the light of the sun began the workday, which lasted from dawn to dusk with a half-hour for breakfast and an hour for lunch.The workers were close-knit families and neighbors, and romance managed to bloom among the teapots.

By the mid nineteenth century electroplated silverware ended the thirty-year dominance of Britannia ware in America and Sheffield plate in England. The first electroplating began in England and France in the 1830s, and a decade later Henry Reed, a pioneer of electroplating in the United States, introduced it at Reed & Barton for distribution to the general public. Reed’s personal experimentation in the electroplate process enabled electroplated silver to be produced on a larger scale than before and was well timed to replace Britannia ware by the 1850s.

Henry Reed and Charles Barton lived next to one another in a two-family tenement on Bay Street, one of a number of houses built by the company in the years from 1840 to 1845. They worked at the bench alongside their employees and were close to the events in their lives. When one of a group of ladies from Taunton visiting the company was surprised to see Barton at his bench, she is said to have exclaimed, “Why, Mr. Barton, I didn’t know you worked!” Barton was close to the workers, a quiet conciliator who was generally not in good health. On 13 September 1867 Barton suffered a stroke on the way home from the factory and died with Reed at his bedside. The closeness of the two men is reflected in the fact that Barton continued to be included in the company’s name after his death.

Over the course of his lengthy career, Reed developed many design and mechanical improvements, such as the use of steel dies with a raised design and a

Above, Silverplated porcelain-lined water pitcher, one of the best-selling items for the company through the 1870s. Reed & Barton archives.

Right, 1891 Taunton Tennis Championship Trophy. Reed & Barton archives.

drop hammer for its application. The operations within the factory were well standardized on a product basis with a high degree of specialization. Reed wanted at least one masterpiece of metal craftsmanship to be in progress at all times as an inspiration.

Seventy-three years after he began work as an eighteen-year-old apprentice, Henry Reed closed the factory door for the last time at age ninety-one. By his death on 1 March 1901, he had seen a new century begin. Henry Reed had more than lived up to the promise of mastering his trade; his company had succeeded in becoming an industry leader known for quality. He established the foundation for those who followed him, and had done so, in his own words, by "just putting one dollar on top of another."

THE REED & BARTON WORKER

When a Reed & Barton burnisher finished off a tray, a fly would break its legs trying to walk across it!

–Employee David Howe, 27 January 1941. Howe developed improved methods of etching, gilding, and polishing.

IT WAS never easy getting a job at Reed & Barton. Henry Reed wanted to know the people he was hiring and made it a point to examine the character and background of each job applicant. He was able to call most of his workers by name and knew much about their personal and family life. The company philosophy was that it was better to have a large number of workers that included part-time than a small number of workers full-time. The number of employees grew from 125 in 1860 to 336 in 1865, 425 in 1871, 500 in 1878, and 800 in 1887. Little escaped the eye of Henry Reed over a career that spanned three-quarters of a century.

No employee was ever discharged because of age. When Joe Martin began work at Reed & Barton in 1903, Harriet Johnson was approaching her ninetieth year. After sixty-four years of employment, Johnson continued to decline the pension offered to her. "I brought this firm up and I propose to stay with it until I die." She fulfilled that wish. Martin recalls, "Every morning she was driven here about 9:30 A.M. As office boy, it was my job to meet her, take her up the elevator, and see that she was safely deposited in her sanctum sanctorum on the third floor. In it was placed a couch, two rocking chairs, a table, and two or three pictures.

"I can see her now, a woman about five feet seven, of slight build, a rather square jaw and hair parted right in the middle and drawn tightly over her ears. She always wore a big white apron. She insisted on rendering some service every day for her compensation. Usually this was hemming the towels that were used in the washrooms. She might do two or three a day. Without question, they were the most expensive towels ever used in any factory in the United States. I have always regretted that we did not frame one. She referred to management by their first names, had positive likes and dislikes concerning the personalities with whom she had worked, and never hesitated to express them."

Silver Room workers. 1909. Reed & Barton archives.

After sixty-four years of employment at Reed & Barton, from 1840 to 1904, Harriet Johnson, a polisher, chose to hem towels for the company rather than accept her pension. "I brought this firm up and I propose to stay with it until I die." Reed & Barton archives.

There was little or no heat in the factory until about 1850, and it is recorded that "the suds and stale beer used in burnishing the ware often froze on the articles and water spilled on a bench or floor remained as ice until the weather allowed it to thaw." Steam heat, first introduced in cotton mills because the cold stiffened the fingers of the operatives and broke the threads, spread to other factories and eventually to homes. The factory was lit by whale-oil lamps, and until 1850 any heat was confined to whale-oil stoves. The working hours were from 5 A.M. to 7 P.M. from March 20 to September 20, with a half-hour off for breakfast at 6:30 A.M. and an hour for dinner at noon. From September 20 to March 20, the hours were from sunrise to 7:30 P.M. and the workers had breakfast before coming to work. Martin remembers working Saturdays until four o'clock.

Wages ranged from apprentices who were paid thirty-one cents per day to the superintendent who was paid two dollars per day. Board was two dollars per week, including meals. Married men were paid, at least in part, by orders at the local stores; and since wages were paid quarterly, the order slips were considered advances to be settled at payment. In industry there were generally few openings for women, but the company needed an increasing supply of workers, and women became a regular part of the work force. Until about 1860 workers kept their own time and work performance accounts.

Seniority rather than productivity determined wages. "A detail in design that might double or triple the cost in a department was not a factor," writes Martin in his memoir, "Reminiscences of the Old Guard." "A young man turning out ten pieces a day, as compared with one of his older associates who produced eight, could not offer the additional 25 percent production as reason for an increase."

The neighborhood surrounding the factory was identified with Reed & Barton. A majority of the dwellings were the homes of workmen, pensioners, families of former employees; almost every house had some personal association with the company. Many of the members of the Taunton Silversmiths Mutual Society, formed in 1893, had been with the company. The presence of cooperative banks, including the Mechanics Cooperative, organized by Reed & Barton employees, helped workers to own housing in the surrounding neighborhood of the factory. "The contribution that this and similar banks have made to the welfare of an industrial community like ours cannot be overestimated," writes Martin in his memoir.

Several members of the same family often worked in the company and sometimes successive generations, which was still rare for this country. In 1855 foreign-born residents in Taunton numbered 3,381 out of a total population of 13,477. The Irish and Canadians became the new hires in the 1880s and 1890s, and Henry Reed showed no favoritism to native Taunton families.

The social life of workers was an extension of the company and included picnics, clambakes, literary societies, debating and political clubs. For one such occasion in September 1848, the Young Whigs invited a speaker from the Midwest. The hall was uncomfortably packed on the very hot night, and Abe Lincoln took off his coat and invited the audience to do the same. The Reed & Barton workers "took to Lincoln immediately" and rallied to demonstrate their loyalty and support at the time of the Civil War. Following his death, the employees at Reed & Barton created a memorial tablet inscribed with the Gettysburg Address.

Foremen were the rulers of their departments from the post-Civil War era to the early twentieth century. They were considered the masters of their trade and their initiative and independence were encouraged. Foreman supremacy, however, could also be overbearing and territorial. They were referred to with a respectful "Mr." and they dressed the part of their authority, reporting for work in silk hats and cutaway coats. They provided the growing number of employees with a rigorous apprenticeship in the Reed & Barton tradition. The retirement of Charles Minchew reflected the foreman's sense of stature and company identity. With his flowing white beard and courtly bearing, Minchew walked on the arm of his son Percy from the plating room to the factory gate past the workers who lined up to applaud him. When he reached the waiting coach, Minchew turned, tipped his hat, and bowed low to his beloved company.

During the nineteenth century, the death of a fellow worker was a solemn occasion. The company closed and everyone came to the funeral, walking in procession by department with mourning bands in the tradition of the old guilds, describes Martin. "Each individual was provided with an arm band of crepe. This was about three inches wide and was worn on the left arm. Those for foremen were different to the extent that small black tassels were hung from them. These arm bands were provided by the company and kept in a special locker till needed. Marshals were appointed and at the head of the line there would be some representation from management and a delegate from each department. Preceding the marchers would be a drummer, sometimes two. Pacing in rhythm with the

Tool makers and machinists. 1908. Reed & Barton archives.

drum beats, the entire organization escorted the body of the departed to its final resting place and then marched back to the plant," relates Martin. "The afflictions of one family were the concern of the neighborhood."

In the years following World War I, the autocratic rule of department foremen was replaced by greater freedom in the workplace accompanied by a shared explanation of managerial changes and objectives. The newly created personnel department replaced foremen in hiring workers. The introduction of standardized wage rates in the 1920s replaced the ritual of bargaining between workman and foreman, and the distinction between the two gradually diminished.

Over the course of the twentieth century, employees formed a company softball team that played in the area Industrial League, enjoyed bowling leagues and golf events, while the Quarter Century Club and Half Century Club organized social gatherings for longtime employees. The minstrel and vaudeville shows performed by employees during the 1950s and the continued civic contribution to the Taunton community illustrate extensions of Reed & Barton activities beyond the factory.

For Director of Personnel Candace Lofgren, Reed & Barton is family. She is the fifth generation of the Dumoulin family to work at Reed & Barton, as are members of the Oldfield, Thurston, and Broomhead families currently employed at the company. Lofgren began in 1967 and is an active member of the company's Quarter Century Club. "I grew up knowing the tremendous respect my family had for Reed & Barton. The company has been a good employer in this town, steady and supportive, with a strong bond to the community. It really makes you feel proud. Retirees still feel a part of the company."

Employees are used to staying a long time, and over the years the camaraderie, shared life experiences, and company activities have meant an avoidance of retirement by many, says Lofgren. "I tell them I am not forcing them to retire, but we have to begin to take out some of their accumulated pension dollars. I have seen so many family members work here, sons who run the same machinery as their fathers had. When I began working, the staff was almost 1,000 and now it is around 400. The biggest problem for our factory workers to accept is seeing manufacturing outsourced to countries where labor is cheaper, such as with stainless steel. What is produced at the Taunton plant remains strong."

Working at the bench with their people, Henry Reed and Charles Barton created an atmosphere of mutual respect between management and employees, re-

Above, Wearing cotton gloves to avoid marring the silver finish, Alonzo "Bonhomme" Dumoulin, assistant plant superintendent, and Arthur Schutzmeister, vice president in charge of production, inspect a coffee pot. 1949. Reed & Barton archives.

Above right, Joseph Desrosiers of the die shop began his career at Reed & Barton in 1900. "My eyes are still keen, my hands are steady, and as long as these remain, I will continue at my bench." 1951. Reed & Barton archives.

lates Sinclair Weeks Jr. With the evolution of a mature factory system and corporate structure, each president depended on the team he developed. "My father Sinclair Weeks, president from 1923 to 1943, understood the need for improved administrative and cost controls and with the help of Treasurer Russell G. Scott made certain they were in place. Arthur Ashworth, a former Colonel of Engineers of the A.E.F.'s 26th Division, was first hired by my father as general manager in 1924 and became president in 1943. Although 'The Colonel' was not experienced or able in the field of marketing, he brought discipline and a tight organization to the factory. Joseph H. Martin was Vice President of Sales; Arthur Schutzmeister the Plant Superintendent; Earl Watson headed Purchasing; and Charles A. Rivard was the Production Manager. There was overlapping continuity between my father's team and that of Ashworth.

"My brother-in-law Roger Hallowell was president from 1953 to 1971, a time of product development and expansion. Working with him were Vice President of Marketing William T. Hurley; Vice President for Retail Sales Matthew H. Bury; Vice President of Manufacturing Gordon B. MacPherson; Treasurer Winthrop B. Wing; Controller William F. C. Maule; Director of Personnel Alvah Dole; Vice President of Merchandising Stafford P. Osborn; President of Eureka Manufacturing Arthur Gebelein; and Assistant Treasurer Norman Dexter.

Veteran spinner Sam Fowler. A flat disc of metal is revolved on a lathe against a chuck or form which has the same shape as the piece to be made. The craftsman forces the metal over the rotating chuck to create the desired shape. 1942. Reed & Barton archives.

"My presidency from 1971 to 1988 faced the challenge of a time of acquisition and change. I relied on the support of Vice President of Administration and Treasurer William H. Dykstra; Vice President of Marketing Richard R. Gillespie; Vice President of Retail Sales Bryce H. Blair; President of Reed & Barton Silversmiths G. Kelvin White; Vice President of Manufacturing and later President of Reed & Barton Silversmiths Henry C. Gill; Vice President of Merchandising Stafford P. Osborn; Controllers William H. Gloekler and Hartley A. Johnson; Director of Personnel John M. Clark; President, Sheffield Silver Company Charles Rodgers; President, Eureka Manufacturing Company Charles P. Terry; and President, Reed & Barton Housewares William Robinson."

Today Al Krebel's presidential team includes Senior Vice President of Finance and Treasurer Charles P. Terry; Senior Vice President of Marketing and Business Development Anthony D. LaChapelle; Vice President of Retail Sales Alan D. Buff; Vice President of Manufacturing James Butcher; Vice President of Administration and Corporate Controller Hartley A. Johnson; Director of Personnel Candace A. Lofgren; Assistant Treasurer Richard Matarese; President of Corporate Markets Harold Anderson; President of Eureka David McLoughlin; President of Miller Rogaska Evangeline Miller; and President of Reed & Barton Housewares William Robinson.

Management may have changed its emphasis over the years, but the essence of the company continues in the quest for quality. When former owner Gustavus Leonard wrote to a customer in 1838, pledging that "we are now taking all pains to give you your 200 *setts* better than any ever has been sent into the market as yet," he spoke for future management as well. Henry Reed set the pace for longevity of employment, a tradition nurtured through the generations. Behind the quality product is the Reed & Barton worker.

1824
REED & BARTON.

YOU CAN'T DO BUSINESS FROM AN EMPTY WAGON

WHEN Vice President of Sales Joseph Martin retired in 1956 after fifty-four years with the company, Sinclair Weeks wrote him a letter of praise that said, "In a closer sense you have been 'Mr. Reed & Barton.' Sales always brings one closer to the people and so in your day-by-day work it must be that you to a greater extent than others have epitomized the shop and its products to our dealers and customers all over the country." His testimonial is a fitting recognition and testament to the essential connection between product and customer.

Joe Martin's sales career at Reed & Barton is a Horatio Alger success story, which began in 1902 when he was hired as an office boy at age thirteen. His formal education may have ended at the eighth grade, but his bent for diplomacy and good personal relationships enabled him to encourage and retain talent during his tenure as vice president of sales from 1939 to1956, a period of marked change in society. A beloved member of the Old Guard, he came of age at the end of the nineteenth century when a sixty- rather than a forty-hour work week was in place at the company. "You came up the hard way and became a master of your profession and established in the community and amongst all your friends an enviable reputation for integrity, character, and high purpose," wrote Weeks. When Martin died in 1959, his close associate William Hurley, vice president of marketing and editor of the company newsletter, *The Silver Lining*, wrote, "No man in the 145 year history of Reed & Barton was better loved and respected or contributed more to the growth and success of the company."

Reed & Barton's display wagon for Taunton's 250th Anniversary Celebration. 1889. Reed & Barton archives.

By the turn of the century, Reed & Barton was already known for its superior sales force, and within the company salesmen were the most highly paid group, exceeding the amount earned by the foremen and department heads. Many sales-

"Hay Meadow Clerks" received their name from the orders they packed in hay for shipment. They kept account of orders, billing, and shipping. Seated in the front row center is Henry Reed's son Frank, and at left of the back row is his nephew Nat Cushman. 1880. Reed & Barton archives.

men began their tenure in the sales department keeping track of orders as "hay meadow clerks" in the packing room where shipments were packed with hay, or as apprentices in the manufacturing department, bringing with them a thorough knowledge of the factory and its products.

As the nation pushed westward so did the Reed & Barton sales force; as "drummers" they were in the vanguard pioneering their own frontier in an expanding nation. There were few comforts in "drumming the trade," which required travel by stagecoach, canal boat, river steamer, horseback, and railroad coaches that were frequently unheated. Frontier business was a speculative gamble as to which prospective customer or another would prosper. The drummers were the company's advertisement and were given great flexibility in courting customers with prices and terms of conditions granted.

Keeping their silver valuables safe was an ever-present concern for salesmen, but when haplessly caught in the midst of a natural disaster, the mettle of the best was sorely tested. The devotion of a Reed & Barton salesman to his product was dramatically illustrated when E. D. Adams was caught in the midst of the San Francisco earthquake in 1906. In his letter to the company on 23 April 1906, Adams conveyed the chaos of the disaster and the extraordinary measures he took to rescue the valuable Reed & Barton silver and keep it safe. Only then did he return home to check on the condition of his wife.

> All that I can say at this writing is, that about 5:15 A.M., Wednesday morning, I was thrown out of bed and in the twinkling of an eye the side of our house was

dashed to the ground. How we got into the street I will never be able to tell, as I fell and crawled down the stairs amid flying glass and timber and plaster. When the dust cleared away I saw nothing but a ruin of a house and home that it had taken twenty years to build. I saw the fires from the city arising in great clouds and it was no time to mourn my loss. . . . Reaching the office, I waded through plaster, etc. to find the goods still in the cases but off the shelves without any damage being done them. Locking the doors again I rushed to the street to find the city two blocks away in flames and the fire department helpless, as all of the water mains had been ruptured and destroyed. I gathered up a force of seven men, stationed them at our office doors, and started for a truck; after hunting an hour I secured a truck at $50.00 a load and again started for the office.

Fortunately I had two guns in the office, and stationing one man at the entrance and one on the truck with orders to shoot, the balance of us went to work. . . . I saved all the Sterling Hollow and Flat Ware with the exception of a few Flat Ware samples in the Trays besides my books, stock sterling, and plated ware books. The plated ware it was impossible to touch, as the flames were then upon us, and another truck at $1000.00 a load was an impossibility. By this time the streets were a pandemonium, and locking office doors we mounted our guarded load and started for the country out toward the Cliff. My house being in ruins I knew not where I would land, but I kept the teamster going with a gun at his back until we were three miles out of town. Meeting a friend, I placed the goods in the parlor of his little cottage that had not been damaged much and I thought I was safe. Then I hiked for home to see how the wife was.

I found her sitting beside the ruins of what was once her home. But she is a brick and never showed the white feather once or since. All Wednesday night we guarded the treasure, but the fire kept creeping toward us, driving the people back to the Cliff House, the western extremity of the Peninsula, and Thursday I was again forced to move the goods westward. The last stand was our backyard, two miles from the first stand, and here I am now with our sterling goods, the remains of a beautiful office. The city is under martial law. . . and as soon as the goods were safe, I cleaned out the nearest grocery store of canned goods and we are living in a tent, cooking meals on a few bricks piled up dutch-oven style. . . . Will endeavor to get into the city tomorrow, but every man caught in town is placed at work clearing the streets and they are kept at work until they drop. With this valuable property under my care I could not afford to take any chances, and I have stayed close to my cache.

One of our prominent attorneys is camped near us and he has advised me that I did the right thing in saving what I could for you, and he says that it will not affect our insurance any and it is only necessary to make an affidavit to what stock we had at the time of fire, and the possibility is that nearly all the insurance companies are broke by this time.

The city is a mass of ruins from the ferry building or waterfront west to Van Ness Ave., and across town from north to south. Within the above radius not a

Heppelwhite Design Sterling Silver Table Ware — *Continued*

	Plain	Engraved
Fish Dish, 25 inches	$123.00	$144.00
Fruit or Flower Basket	128.00	135.00
Gravy Boat	42.00	51.00
Gravy Boat Tray	19.00	24.00
Ice Cream Plates, per dozen	144.00	192.00
Ice Cream Platter	72.00	91.00
Meat Dish, 16 inches	75.00	94.00
Meat Dish, 18 inches	102.00	123.00
Meat Dish, 20 inches	134.00	158.00
Sandwich Tray	42.00	51.00
Tea Strainer	6.75	8.75
Vegetable Dish, double, 10 inches	99.00	112.00
Vegetable Dish, open, 11 inches	42.00	49.00
Waiter, No. 740, 26 inches	270.00	305.00
Water Pitcher, capacity 7 half pints	96.00	112.00

Heppelwhite Design, Sterling Silver Tea Set, No. 560
Waiter, No. 740, 26 inches

44

Prices of Nickel Silver Articles

Asparagus Dishes	$15.50 to $30.00
Baking Dishes	21.50 to 30.00
Bottle Stands	3.00 to 13.00
Bread Trays and Baskets	6.75 to 19.00
Breakfast Casters, small, 3-bottle	6.50 to 8.00
Butter Dishes	13.50 to 20.00
Plates, individual, per dozen	10.00 to 24.00
Candelabra, per pair	50.00 upwards
Candlesticks, per pair	15.00 to 35.00
Chafing Dishes	28.00 to 65.00

Nickel Silver Tea Set, No. 5045

Tea Set, 5 pieces	$110.00
Kettle to match	45.00
Waiter to match, 24 inches	75.00

113

Above, Sterling silver tableware, *Heppelwhite* design, and *right*, nickel silver articles from the 1913–14 Reed & Barton catalogue. Reed & Barton archives.

business house is left standing. Dohrmann Commercial Co., Shreve & Co., every jeweler are a thing of the past. Not a hotel in town, restaurant or café.

As all of our photo books were destroyed, I would request that you forward me a line as soon as possible. N. S. Hollow and W. M. Hollow hotel photos, and regular W. M. stock photos. Address E. H. Adams, #151–24th Avenue, San Francisco, Cal. W. F. Express.

Will start in and make out a list of what I saved in Sterling and forward it immediately, so that you may present your claim under your insurance policies that you have at the factory.

Trusting that what I have done will meet with your approval, I remain,

Yours truly,
Sgd. E. D. Adams.

Here we are all paupers together, but we have our grit left.

Assigned to Oklahoma, then known as Indian Territory, Paul Storm Sr. began his long sales career in 1901, "when the city of Tulsa didn't have a single paved street. That was pioneering at its best. I was the first representative of any silver company in Indian Territory. My initial trip lasted 11 weeks and official net sales came to $1,700. Business was wonderful! All traveling then was done by train and salesmen often rode in the caboose of mile-long freights to get where they wanted because passenger train service didn't accommodate their schedule," recalls Storm. In 1904 Storm was asked to move to Texas and develop the company's business there. The Lone Star State and the lone Reed & Barton salesman took to one another with legendary success.

Joe Martin saw in the Reed & Barton salesman, the kernel of the company's success. He optimistically planned for increases in product lines based on his conviction that a good team could always sell more next year. Conservative in approach, Martin's pride in Reed & Barton's existing product lines, such as the company's reputation for high-quality plated holloware, led him to ignore the lifestyle changes toward casual entertaining. Neither did he embrace the potential of stainless steel flatware as a future growth area for the company, while in sterling flatware he integrated well the combined strategies of market research, new pattern introduction, effective advertising, and promotion.

Former Vice President of Sales Matthew Bury would arrive to work at Reed & Barton still wearing his Taunton High School Cadet Corps uniform. He was eight-

Above, Vice President of Sales Joseph Martin is honored at his retirement in 1956 by Chairman of the Board Sinclair Weeks; and *below*, with President Roger Hallowell.

een and 1929 was the year of the big stock market crash. He pursued college in the evening, happy to have a job at Reed & Barton, the dominant industry in Taunton. "I worked as an apprentice in the silversmithing and plating departments for twenty-five cents an hour and then went to the cost-accounting department where I compared the price of the product to the cost of manufacturing it. During the depression years the philosophy of General Manager Arthur Ashworth was, 'Let's keep the plant going. How much work can we give the staff?' We made many things on a promotional basis to supply work. There were few layoffs in the factory; it was an opportunity to progress and learn. If you had a job you were happy. Workers developed responsibility, a loyalty to the company."

Happy as Bury was to have a job during the depression, he found himself working seven days a week on sales department correspondence and promotional literature, and he finally convinced Ashworth of the need to hire someone to do marketing and advertising. In 1933 William Hurley was hired as advertising manager and the two worked closely as an effective sales and marketing management team. "Bill Hurley was a good writer, worked well with the advertising agencies, and knew how to arrange a good deal with the newspapers."

Bury initiated the first contact for Hagerty polish, convinced of its merits following a meeting with Nelson Page, a silver buyer for Jaccard Jewelry in Kansas City in 1959. Bill and Pat Hagerty were country boys from South Bend, Indiana, who were making the cleaner in their garage from a formula created by their grandfather. Hagerty Silver Foam had been sold door-to-door since 1895 with the entire family traveling for months at a time. When they arrived in a city, the polish would be mixed in a bathtub, and as children the Hagerty brothers would help spoon it into gallon jars.

Attempts were made to distribute the polish through retail stores, but by the time of the Hagerty brothers' meeting in 1959 with William T. Hurley, then vice president of marketing, they were looking for representation by a leading silver manufacturer to ensure sufficient sales. Hagerty polish had been used at the White House for many years and subsequent tests proved the polish to be even superior to Reed & Barton's own. In 1958 a group of national women's magazines judged Hagerty Silver Foam superior to ninety-six other brands of polish and urged its national distribution. Reed & Barton financed their operation and its sales force was able to put the Hagerty name on the global map, enabling the company to achieve the largest share of the silver polish market in the United States.

Vice President of Marketing William Hurley (pictured above), and Vice President of Retail Sales Matthew Bury were an effective management team during their long careers at Reed & Barton. 1970. Photographs courtesy of the Reed & Barton archives and Matt Bury.

In 1970 Bury became vice president of the company's retail sales division and during his forty-seven-year career experienced the transition from the jeweler as the company's main customer to the department and specialty stores. "My major accounts were J. E. Caldwell in Philadelphia; Shreve, Crump & Low of Boston; Macy's in New York; J. B. Hudson & Son, jewelers in Minneapolis; C. D. Peacock, a prominent independent jeweler in Chicago; Linz Brothers, jewelers in Dallas; and Marshall Field in Chicago. I remember James Raleigh, the buyer for Marshall Field who only allowed our people to call him Jim."

In his fifty-two years at Reed & Barton, Craig Francis, sales representative, New England territory, exemplified the company sales force in style and care of customers and has appropriately reached his emeritus years silver haired with distinction. "In some years he earned more than I did as president, and he deserved it," says Sinclair Weeks Jr. "On a Christmas Eve he might still be making sure deliveries reached his customers." Francis has been one of the few individuals to be named Salesman of the Year more than once, a coveted company award based on multi criteria. His long tenure has also meant serving as dean of the sales force, a tradition at Reed & Barton that offers mentoring and guidance to newer sales people.

Reed & Barton has been a family affair for Francis. "My grandfather worked here; my father was a foreman for the silversmiths and worked here for over forty years; my brother was superintendent of maintenance and had been with the company also for over forty years." Francis began traveling for the company in 1948. "It was a tough road show. There was lack of sleep and constant moving. In the earlier years I used to travel by train, bringing a ton of merchandise for trunk shows at hotels through New York, Pennsylvania, Maryland, and Delaware, covering the cities of Syracuse, Rochester, Buffalo, Pittsburgh, Harrisburg, and York. We'd fill a room with goods and work the crowd like we were doing a show. Then it was packing the trunk to go on to another hotel to do it all over again." The sampling of merchandise was extensive and heavy, with sterling meat platters, water pitchers, hand-chased *Francis I* pieces, and tea sets. "At one time we had twenty-eight tea sets in the active line. There would be three wall cases and three floor cases full. I brought such a huge array of silver with me that when I got through, I never saw a salesman to compete with. I went home every three weeks, took a week off, and started out again."

With a low turnover, Reed & Barton offered appealing continuity with their sales people, which gave them a competitive advantage that became a standard

1796 200th 1996
Tables by: Lee Bierly & Christopher Drake Tim Callis Abby Camp Sandra Fairbanks
Jeffrey Fishbein Mollie Johnson Gary McBournie Kevin Musumano Alex Pappas Marie Piraino
Manuel de Santaren Charles Spada Michael Tavano Lisa Vandenburgh Peter Wheeler
Come watch Boston's best designers do battle armed with little more than forks, knives and spoons.
What topic could they possibly be facing off over? We thought the tines up/tines down controversy was all but decided. Ah, of course, it's our annual Festive Table celebration, a sterling entertainment to be sure.
Every year at this time, we enlist the talents of Boston's best designers to decorate, nay, bedazzle 15 holiday tables in our store. How do we choose the best? With the assistance of Cheryl and Jeffrey Katz. And, while the results are wonderfully unpredictable, the choice of silverware is most predictably biased toward Reed & Barton. (Two artisans in sterling who possessed an admirable knack for setting the table.) And, considering the wealth of Reed & Barton pieces that will be displayed, even Queen Elizabeth might feel compelled to take an impromptu inventory at the Tower.
If past years are any indication, hosts and hostesses look forward to this event with a childlike anticipation usually reserved for dessert. Not all of us, after all, find sufficient decorating inspiration in a glue gun. If you've been given the charge of entertaining this season, we encourage you to reserve room on your social calendar to attend. Come, pick up a fork (in a pleasing pattern, say Francis I) and join the fray. This battle will be fought and won in the dining room. As history has taught us, the one who leaves with the most silver wins.
Dessert by Jean Claude Perennou of Ambrosia on Huntington
18th Century
Burgundy
Golden Ashmont
English Chippendale
Francis I
Grande Renaissance
THE FESTIVE TABLE:
A STERLING CELEBRATION
Featuring Reed & Barton Silver
November 7 to November 23, 1996
Sterling Silver
The Eternal Element of Style
SHREVE, CRUMP & LOW
REED & BARTON
Two floors. And who knows how many stories.
330 Boylston Street, Boston • The Mall at Chestnut Hill • (617) 267-9100 • For information, call 800 324-0222
Our Boston Store Hours are 10:00 am to 5:30 pm, Monday through Saturday

in the industry. "We have never lost a salesman to a competitor," says Francis. He remembers salesmen like Paul Storm Sr., who had pioneered effectively for Reed & Barton "everything west of the Mississippi to the Rockies. He would take two truckloads of merchandise out for two to three months. The territory belonged to him."

Strong relationships with dealers enabled salesmen like Francis to put the company's line in their store. "Shelf space is everything. When we introduced new pattern designs, we created a market, which would spark a related tabletop product such as a china pattern. Business was done on a very personal basis, with store owners inviting you home for dinner and to stay overnight. Today business is driven by cost. During most of my career there was no foreign competition, and sterling flatware was the mainstay of the company's business, enabling my volume to be very substantial."

The golden time for Francis was when the jeweler used to be the salesman's major customer. It was a time of white gloves and a presentation of your offerings on a white placemat. "The buyer in the jewelry store knew who he was selling to. I remember when the entire rear of Shreve, Crump & Low was silver."

Hagerty silver polish was a good volume seller for Francis particularly after tarnish test demonstrations. "An eight-ounce jar cost just two dollars and I was selling it by the tractor-trailer load. At twelve jars in a carton I was walking through the stock. Then television picked it up and I was averaging $5,000 a week in sales."

Darryl Nelson, sales representative for the Minnesota/Midwest territory, came to Reed & Barton in 1982 after previously working for the Towle Company for fifteen years. He explains that the tabletop business is close knit, with a lot of related associations. "There was always great respect for Reed & Barton. The company still has that uniqueness; you can feel the history. Sinny traveled through my Midwest territory with me in 1983. We followed the Lewis and Clark trail and I got him a cowboy hat that made him look like Wild Bill Hickok. He's a classic. The jewelers always loved the Weeks family and Sinny has great respect in the industry.

"Selling silver used to be a country club atmosphere with party gala events, trunk shows, and dealers invited to your hotel room, and six weeks' travel by train. We used to do a teaspoon promotion for a dollar to encourage buyers to register for a pattern. Today buying is price driven and only 5 to 8 percent of the

Advertisement for Shreve, Crump & Low's 200th anniversary features display of Reed & Barton sterling silver. *Boston Globe Magazine*, 27 October 1997. Courtesy of Shreve, Crump & Low.

Attendees at sales convention in the summer of 1980 gather in front of Reed & Barton's silver doors. President Sinclair Weeks Jr. seated front row center. Reed & Barton archives.

Above, Senior Vice President of Marketing and Business Development Anthony LaChapelle. "The style of earlier salesmen has left a feeling of integrity, a consistency in the way of doing business." 1998. Reed & Barton archives.

Below, Vice President of Retail Sales Alan Buff. "Fifty percent of the company's business is still with retail jewelers and specialty tabletop stores." 1998. Reed & Barton archives.

population buy sterling. When sterling flatware was 85 percent of the company's core business, you were able to have complementary holloware. Today stainless is the biggest product category for the consumer." The total number of retailers has dwindled because of the growth of mail order catalogues and home shopping on television, he says. "A lot of jewelers don't have tabletop products anymore. The overhead is higher for them, but the jeweler had great product knowledge."

"Fifty percent of the company's business is still with retail jewelers and specialty tabletop stores," relates Vice President of Retail Sales Alan Buff. "There are customers who desire, expect, and are willing to pay for a higher level of service. Department stores by economic necessity have reduced their level of service, and their very identity has been impacted by acquisition and consolidation."

Department stores offer their own opportunities. "They produce glamorous catalogues that come out regularly and present the product very favorably," says Buff. "And because it is the retailer's presentation and preference, the ad provides reinforcement and a level of credibility to the consumer. If Neiman Marcus or Bloomingdales carries and promotes the product, it must be good."

The many branches of a department store permit a wide outreach and accessibility for products. In today's mobile society, items included on bridal registries, for example, are available to guests coming from varied locations to the wedding. Nor can you compete with the display space of department stores, observes Buff. "They are our showrooms, familiarizing consumers with the product, allowing them the chance to touch and feel. Such first-hand knowledge in turn has given the consumer the confidence to order from catalogues and has promoted the direct mail business."

Ross-Simons is an example of a catalogue business that has evolved to present a luxury image and has benefited from the inclusion of national brands like Reed & Barton. It has become one of the ten most prominent tabletop businesses and includes a growing chain of retail stores, observes Buff. "The American consumer has less time to shop and is doing more business with four color catalogues."

Salesmen carry fewer samples than their predecessors did, and trunk shows have been replaced with regional trade exhibits that display the breadth of product line. "Our sales force," says Buff, "is focused on detail, service, and support work, making sure that the product is on display and the sales staff has the necessary knowledge to provide the required information."

Partial Account Listing

Coleman E. Adler & Sons
Eddie Bauer
L.L. Bean
Bed, Bath & Beyond
Belk Stores
Bloomingdale's
The Bon Marché
Borsheim's
Bromberg & Company, Inc.
Burdine's
Byron Cade
Dayton's-Hudson's-Marshall Field's
Dillard's
Michael C. Fina
Famous-Barr
Filene's
Foley's
Fortunoff's
Geary's
Gump's
Hall's
Hecht's
Heslop's China & Gifts
House of 1776
Irish Cottage
Kaufmann's
Meier & Frank
Macy's East
Macy's West
Neiman Marcus
J.C. Penney
QVC
Reading China & More
Rich's-Lazarus-Goldsmith's
Robinsons-May
Rocky's Gold & Silver
Ross-Simons
Michael Round Fine China & Crystal, Inc.
Nat Schwartz & Company
Schwarzchild Jewelers
Shreve, Crump & Low
The Silver Store
Thurber's
George Watts & Son, Inc.

Today Reed & Barton's twenty-two person sales force can more easily traverse the country. There are fewer customers to see within a geographic area, but each contributes a greater share of the business. Retailers are specialized in the products they carry and can select from Reed & Barton, in addition to silver, the extensive line of products that includes crystal, porcelain, stainless steel, wooden chests, humidors, and licensed products under the names of Ralph Lauren and Waterford. It was Henry Reed who said, "You can't do business from an empty wagon," and today's Reed & Barton sales force "drums" a more expansive trade.

The last two decades, observes Senior Vice President of Marketing and Business Development Tony LaChapelle, have been a time of outreach for the company in developing a broad product and price line that has tested different venues. In such a time of transition, the importance of the sales force is evident, as diverse buyers are needed for the variety of products offered. "Our sales force has given us a sustainable competitive advantage and has been one of our biggest assets. It has also enabled us to survive in difficult years. Our sales people stay with us. In the trade the word has been if you can get to Reed & Barton, you have reached the best. The style of earlier salesmen has left a feeling of integrity, a consistency in the way of doing business."

MINNESOTA
PRESENTED TO THE
BATTLESHIP MINNESOTA
BY THE STATE OF
MINNESOTA
1909

THE MANUFACTURER MEETS THE PUBLIC

THE EARLY history of Reed & Barton was focused on production and the machinery that made it possible. Henry Reed, devoted to fine craftsmanship, continued to be absorbed in the technical matters of the factory and product design. Following the prosperity of the Civil War years, manufacturers found it necessary to devote increasing attention to marketing the products they were able to produce.

George Brabrook was a man who could sell. His administration at Reed & Barton spanned the forty years from 1860 to 1900. It was Brabrook who was responsible for the company's marketing and who regarded quality as its basic selling appeal. Reed & Barton would not concede quality as secondary to price because of his conviction that low cost at the expense of quality was poor economy.

George Brabrook had a thorough knowledge of design and salesmanship and, like Charles Barton and Henry Reed, was a visible manager at the factory. "He was often seen dashing at top speed across the yard from office building to factory and back, a stub of pencil in one hand, an order book in the other." Brabrook had the intuitive ability to sense what the market wanted. Through his guidance a product design department was created and in 1873 the first specialist and full-time designer, W. C. Beattie from England, was hired. By 1889 twenty-four men were working in the design department, and Brabrook had guided the company's entry into the manufacture of sterling silver.

Growth in the nation's population and the railroad as a source of transporting products created new markets and the competition among businesses to reach them. Companies displayed their products at exhibitions and fairs and vied for coveted medals and awards. It was the course favored by Brabrook who engaged in limited media advertising.

Sterling bowl commissioned for the battleship USS *Minnesota* and presented by the people of the state of Minnesota in 1909. Reed & Barton made large sterling services for a number of battleships, financed by donations from people of their respective states. Reed & Barton archives.

George Brabrook, 1828–1908, guided the company's entry into the manufacture of sterling silver in 1889. During his forty-year career from 1860 to 1900, he excelled in sales and design, insisting on quality as Reed & Barton's selling appeal. Reed & Barton archives.

Opposite page, above, Roman Medallion tea set. 1868. Collection of Robert H. Bury.

Left, Silverplated flatware, *Roman Medallion.* The first original Reed & Barton flatware pattern was designed by Henry Reed, made in silverplate, and patented in December 1868. Each utensil had its own distinctive Roman headdress. Collection of Robert H. Bury.

Right, Close-up of the Roman warrior helmets. Collection of Robert H. Bury.

The growth of flatware was closely tied to hotel ware. Flatware was primarily manufactured for the hotel trade and until 1868 Reed & Barton produced six to eight patterns common to the trade. In December 1868 the first original Reed & Barton flatware pattern, *Roman Medallion,* was designed and patented by Henry Reed. Considerations of price, use, and care resulted in a minimum of decoration for most hotel patterns. The ornate design of the *Gem, Pearl, Unique, Orient,* and *Brilliant* patterns, introduced over the next decade by the company, may well have been intended for household use.

All Reed & Barton flatware was silverplated on a base metal of high quality nickel silver, deposited in four different grades of thickness. The nickel silver alloy contained the hard white metal nickel along with copper and zinc. A dozen teaspoons in the *Roman Medallion* pattern ranged from $4.25 for Extra Plate to $5.25 for Double Plate, to $6.25 for Triple Plate, to $7.25 for Quadruple Plate. Extra heavy spoons in plain patterns for hotel and steamboat use were priced from $5.75 per dozen for Extra Plate to $9.50 for Quadruple Plate.

Manufacturers competed with one another in the variety of flatware produced, so that almost every type of food appeared to have a piece of flatware designed for it. In 1880, for example, Reed & Barton manufactured twenty different varieties of spoons, twelve different forks, and ten different knives, with the complete flatware line consisting of fifty-seven different items. Most of the pieces were made in four grades and in more than a dozen patterns.

The Philadelphia Centennial Exhibition of 1876 included a five-month-long demonstration in Fairmont Park of arts and manufacturing, eliciting unprecedented public interest. People arrived from all over the nation and visitors came worldwide to the exhibition halls. For the first time the American manufacturer was face-to-face with his market. Reed & Barton's display cabinet, nineteen feet long and eleven feet high, included 1,040 gilded and silverplated items. Exhibit expenses for the company cost $15,250.

Each manufacturer prepared a spectacular centerpiece. The *Progress Vase,* submitted by Reed & Barton's head designer W. C. Beattie for the company, received a medal for excellence and elicited considerable praise from viewers. The hand-carved sculpture presents the allegorical figure of Progress as a winged female. A scenic relief panel portrays the discovery of America. To the left is a representation of the nineteenth century. Liberty is on horseback surrounded by emblems of Prosperity, and two children display emblems of Arts and Sciences.

The urn is flanked on the right by a representation of the fifteenth century that includes two Indians, one on horseback, traversing uncultivated terrain and threatened by a rattlesnake. The three presentations are mounted on a molded base with plaques inscribed "AMERICA," "XIX CENTURY," and "XV CENTURY." The silverplated sculpture stands four feet long and three feet high and illustrates the progress of centuries towards peace and enlightenment.

The *Progress Vase* is on display in the main foyer at Reed & Barton. On rare occasions it is loaned for display, such as at the Chicago World's Fair (1933–34); at Macy's department store in New York City during "Reed & Barton Week" in April 1955; at the nation's bicentennial exhibit at the Smithsonian Institution in Washington, D.C.; and most recently in 1996 at Shreve, Crump & Low for its two hundredth anniversary.

Reed & Barton's participation at the Philadelphia Centennial Exhibition was judged a success based on the favorable public comment and resulting sales. A tea set of electroplate on display, heavily decorated with repoussé chasing and gilt, was purchased by members of the Japanese Commission for the Emperor of Japan. "Chasing" is hand decoration applied with small tools and punches. When flowers and scrolls are impressed into the flat surface, it is called "flat chasing." When the ornamentation is brought up into high relief by driving out

The Reed & Barton display case at the Centennial Exhibition, Philadelphia, 1876. The dramatic *Progress Vase*, designed for the Centennial, is in the left-hand side of the case. Reed & Barton archives.

the metal from the inside and then molded into detailed form, it is called "repoussé" or "raised chasing."

In 1976, during the nation's bicentennial, Reed & Barton received a letter from John Percy McAdams of Virginia, the grandson of a couple who were courting at the time of the Philadelphia Centennial Exhibition and much admired the repoussé tea set purchased for the Emperor of Japan. The couple married later that year and received as a treasured wedding gift the repoussé tea service just like the one they had seen at the Exhibition. Their grandson, who had inherited the tea set, offered the service to the Smithsonian Institution for the bicentennial exhibit appropriately entitled "1876: A Centennial Exhibition." In a replay of history, the *Progress Vase* was also on display as it had been in his grandparents' day.

Without illustrative materials, trade was limited to markets where sample lines could be shown to customers. Advertising the company's products through newspapers faced the technical limitations of photographic reproduction at the time. The development of illustrated catalogues was therefore significant in the marketing history of Reed & Barton. Electrotypography had made large-scale commercial application of wood engravings available and the illustrated catalogue possible. Salesmen recognized that customers wanted catalogues for their own use, as one such letter to the factory relates. "These people all ask for books. They need a book to which a ready reference can be had to anything you make."

Reed & Barton's first catalogue, "in the grand manner," appeared in 1877, was 224 pages in length, and contained fine woodcuts that were one-third the actual size of the line. In 1885 Reed & Barton produced an outstanding catalogue that remains impressive over a century later for its undertaking and content. The 1885 catalogue, fourteen inches by seventeen inches, contains 400 pages of almost 4,000 wood engravings and a steel-engraved frontispiece of the Reed & Barton factory. There are four color lithographic plate pages of the company's products. All engravings are half the actual size of the products and each book weighs sixteen pounds. Reed & Barton craftsmen made the wood engravings, a project that employed twenty-seven engravers for three years. Seven thousand volumes were printed and distributed to customers at a cost exceeding $100,000.

By 1880 Taunton had a population of 25,448 and was no longer an isolated community dependent on river transportation. The New Bedford Railroad and the Taunton branch connection to Boston had been supplemented by the Old Colony branch lines to Fall River and to Boston. The Fall River Line operated the

XIX CENTURY
AMERICA
XV CENTURY

Left, The *Progress Vase.* Awarded first prize at the Centennial Exhibition, Philadelphia, 1876, the four-foot-long, three-foot-high statuary symbolized progress, from conquering a hostile environment in the fifteenth century to attaining peace and enlightenment in the nineteenth century. The *Progress Vase* is on display in the entrance hall of Reed & Barton.

Right, Close-up of the groupings of the *Progress Vase.*

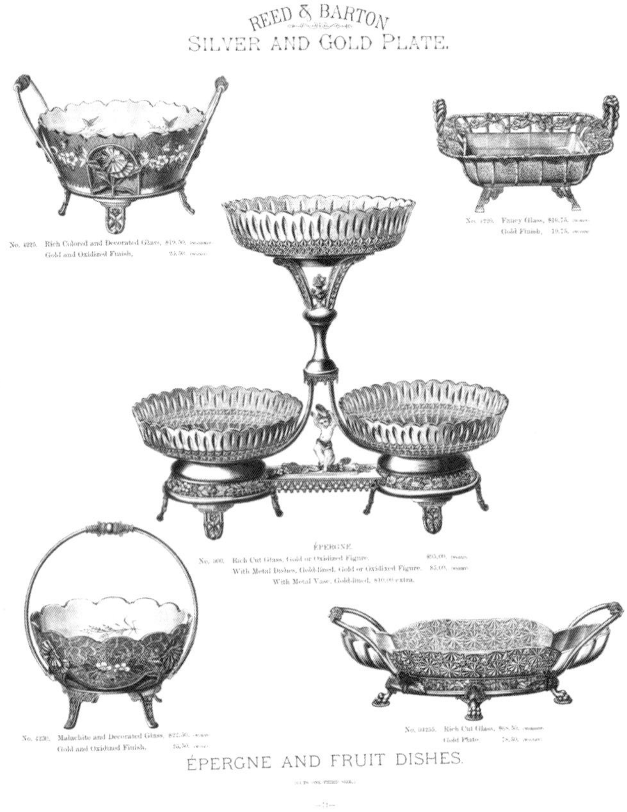

Display of epergne, fruit dishes, and tureens from the 1885 Reed & Barton catalogue. Reed & Barton archives.

two luxurious steamboats, the *Bristol* and the *Providence,* which were efficient means for handling freight. The telegraph cable could communicate with world markets. The major streets were paved, new houses built, including a number of mansions on Dean Street; and stores and factories reflected the general prosperity of expansive trade nationwide.

Yet the hay meadow clerks continued to prepare company wares for shipping as their fathers had, and Davenport & Mason wagons still came to the company yard each evening to take their daily load of crates and barrels to market. With the growth of department stores, a natural competition arose with the independent retail jewelers. Initially large manufacturers like Reed & Barton favored the jewelers and did not sell to department stores, but over time department stores built their own reputation for quality.

The "new and better product" was sterling silver. The word "sterling" came from a group of merchants associated with the cities around the Baltic Sea, known as the Easterlings, and the silver which they brought into England was always of a fixed quality and everyone knew what a pound of Easterling silver was worth. The standard that sterling must contain 92.5 percent pure silver was set in 1335, and for centuries the penalty was death for including any less. Until the Civil War period solid silver, beyond an occasional coin-silver spoon, was generally inaccessible to the mass market and the producers were craftsmen rather than manufacturers.

The Comstock Lode discovered in 1859 was in peak production by the mid 1870s and new mines increased the supply of silver. Improved metallurgical processes decreased costs of production and enabled lower-grade ores to be used. As silver prices declined, the differential between sterling flatware and the high end of silverplated flatware lessened. The luxurious silver services of the mining barons created their own romance, and sterling silver became the accepted gift for weddings.

Reaching out to new customers, George Brabrook began the manufacture and sale of sterling silver products in 1889. The power press of the factory displaced the hand hammer of the workshop. Sterling was an appropriate expression of the company's ideals of fine craftsmanship and quality. Brabrook's initiative was correct and the new line performed well immediately. Sterling sales rose from $66,055 in 1890 to $217,950 in 1891 and to $312,005 in 1892. By 1900 an entire factory building at Reed & Barton was used for the manufacture of sterling.

With population growth came the problems of how to serve a widening mar-

William Bradford Homer Dowse, 1852–1928, seated in center, at an outing with foremen. Dowse brought financial experience and strength of leadership to the company. 1920. Reed & Barton archives.

ket. Despite the successful hotel trade, sales of electroplated flatware and holloware had been in decline since 1880. The widespread depression of 1893 resulted in business failures and four years of economic depression. The struggle for sales in the industry ignored established price levels and trade practices. In the latter part of 1898, the consolidation of sixteen silver companies, including the Meriden Britannia Company, Rogers & Bros., and Holmes & Edwards, to form the International Silver Company presented Reed & Barton and the industry with a potent competitor and one able to control over 75 percent of the electroplate manufacturing in the nation. All branches of the silver industry were included in the International merger from inexpensive low quality "flash" plate to sterling silver. It was one way of dealing with growth of markets and represented the opposite of specialization.

The challenge was great for Reed & Barton to maintain its position faced with the diversification of International and the high-end specialization of the Gorham Manufacturing Company in sterling and expensive electroplate. But the Reed & Barton name stood for quality, and by the turn of the century the company was competing with the best in the world.

When Henry Reed died in 1901, his son-in-law William B. H. Dowse became president. Following his marriage to Fanny Reed in 1883, Dowse had already begun to handle Reed & Barton's legal affairs. Though temperamentally different, Reed and Dowse respected each other's abilities. The growing complexities of business called less for mechanical than financial abilities, which many manufacturers lacked. Dowse, who graduated from Harvard College and Harvard Law School, brought financial talent and organizational abilities.

As a patent lawyer, he became interested in manufacturing enterprises, particularly the development of a snap fastener, based upon the ball and socket, to replace the button and hole. He became treasurer and acquired sufficient capital to obtain control of the Consolidated Fastener Company, of Boston, and continued to run this enterprise while president of Reed & Barton.

His formidable personal appearance, imposing frame, moustache and goatee created a dignified but haughty demeanor, accompanied by a booming voice and autocratic and impatient temperament. It was a contrast to the quiet manner of Reed, Barton, and Brabrook. But his frankness and adherence to his word won respect. His vigor energized the company. He moved quickly and with confidence.

Equipment was updated including the introduction of electric lights and plumbing. Modern-designed turbines replaced the old water wheels. Changes were made in the transmission of power and a coupling arranged by which either water or steam power could be used independently of the other.

Management consultants analyzed production and overhead costs, and "costs" for the first time were used to set prices. The attempt was to make production and management more scientific in their functioning. The unit cost of doing business was lowered as the volume increased, and the sales force was aggressively promoted. Dowse was applying in Taunton the forces that were making America a great industrial nation.

William Bradford Homer Dowse succeeded his father-in-law, Henry Reed, as president from 1901 to 1923. Reed & Barton archives.

Unlike Brabrook, Dowse favored mass production and a wide distribution of goods. When Dowse attempted to introduce in 1911 a less expensive holloware line, he found that Henry Reed had trained his workers too well. The Reed & Barton tradition of craftsmanship knew only one way to solder or buff and defeated any efforts to lower production costs.

While Henry Reed and George Brabrook had drawn up plans for a company-operated retail store in 1894, Dowse put them into effect. In 1902 a New York subsidiary corporation was established, and the Reed & Barton Company, of

Interior of Reed & Barton's Fifth Avenue Store, 4 Maiden Lane, corner of Fifth Avenue and Thirty-second Street, New York, 1905–1918. Reed & Barton archives.

The elegance of sterling design is displayed with the 1899 pattern *Love Disarmed.* Reed & Barton archives.

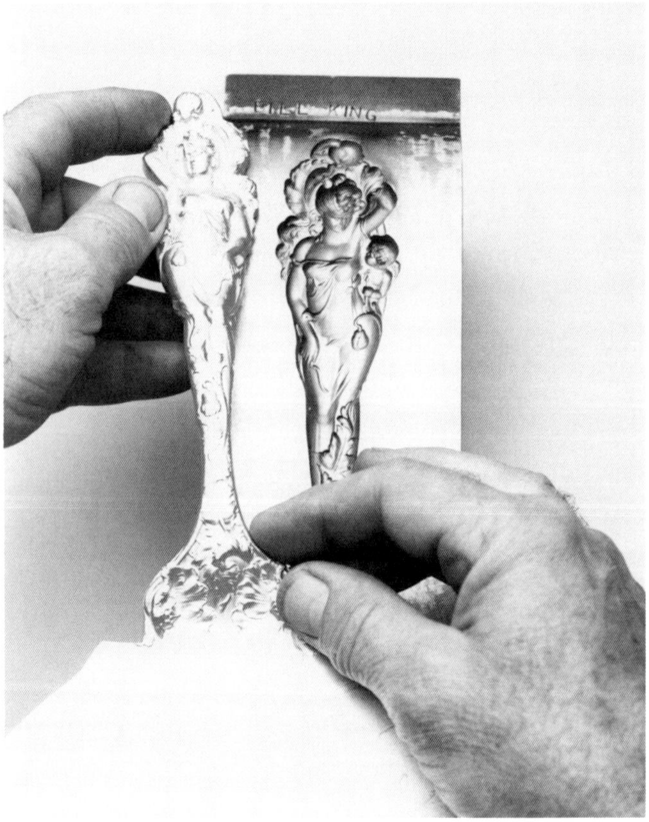

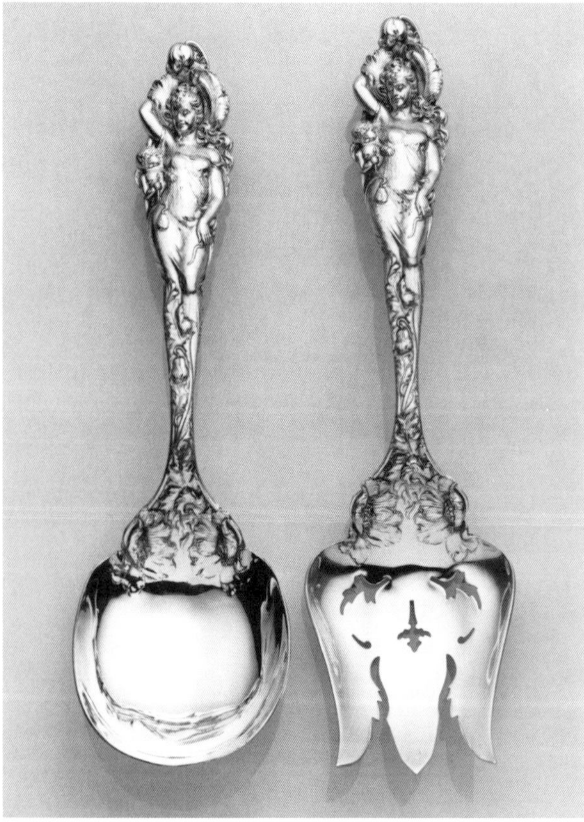

New York, took over the leases of the Maiden Lane and Union Square wholesale offices. In 1905 the company opened a large retail store on the corner of Fifth Avenue and Thirty-second Street, a luxurious showcase that was the trophy of the Dowse administration.

Reed & Barton's modern advertising began in 1905 with the opening of the New York store. A descriptive pamphlet accompanied each new sterling flatware pattern, and in 1914 catalogues were issued for the main product line. This material was supplemented by advertising in the nation's leading monthly periodicals, and prepared cuts and copy were provided to dealers for use in local newspapers. The 1924 centennial of the company occasioned extensive advertising, and thousands of replicas of the company's first pewter cream pitcher were manufactured for distribution in the trade.

Other silverware manufacturers had already established retail stores in New York. But there was strong opposition from retail jewelers to competing manufacturer-operated stores. The store at 320 Fifth Avenue was an expensive investment and too close to the garment industry for the uptown trade, but in the field of quality merchandising Reed & Barton competed for thirteen years with the best jewelry and silverware shops in the city.

In 1918 Reed & Barton purchased control of the well-known jewelry store of Theodore B. Starr, Inc., at 576 Fifth Avenue and introduced the company line by merging with the Starr organization and the use of its name. But jewelry did not sufficiently attract silverware buyers and the retail experiment ended in 1924.

The trophy line expanded, bringing with its special orders valued advertising for the company. Indeed, Reed & Barton, the Gorham Manufacturing Company, and Tiffany & Company dominated the trophy trade. Dowse sought the edge by introducing in 1910 a commercial line of ready-made sterling cups that placed silver trophies within the means of smaller clubs and built a substantial volume of business. Handsome sterling services were made for the battleships *Arizona, California, Minnesota, Montana, South Dakota,* and *Utah.*

When President William Howard Taft signed the bill for Arizona to become the forty-eighth state on 14 February 1912, L. W. Mix, the mayor of Nogales, began a campaign to honor the occasion with the naming of a United States battleship. On 13 March 1913, the day Woodrow Wilson was inaugurated president, the ship received Congressional authorization, and the USS *Arizona* was launched at the Brooklyn Navy Yard on 19 June 1915. In 1916, the year the *Arizona* began active service, the state's Board of Trade selected Reed & Barton to produce a silver ser-

Selections from the silver service produced for the USS *Arizona. Clockwise from left,* A water pitcher sits upon a glass serving tray. An engraving of the Casa Grande Ruins is depicted below the water pitcher's spout, and a stylized dolphin forms the water pitcher's handle.

The coffee urn was one of the most frequently used items before the set was retired from use. A stylized dolphin forms the lid's handle. The front of the urn reads, "Presented to the USS Arizona by the People of the State of Arizona 1916," and a University of Arizona building is displayed on the back.

The dramatic centerpiece bowl has garland bordered engravings portraying the Carnegie Laboratory and a Gila monster, while Neptune figures ride on dolphins with shells and anchors.

Courtesy of the Arizona State Capitol Museum, a Division of the Arizona Department of Library, Archives and Public Records.

vice, because of the company's reputation for quality and the creation of similar silver pieces for many United States ships.

The campaign to raise the $9,000 required to pay for the silver service was a state-wide event and even school children donated pennies. Memorial Day and July Fourth were designated as Tag Days, when students throughout Arizona sold tags to raise money for the silver.

To inspire contributions, Reed & Barton began producing silver pieces which were displayed in major towns and gave the people of Arizona the chance to see the silver before it was placed on the battleship. An elegant eighty-seven piece sterling service was produced for the ship's commanding officers, some with copper plating over sterling to recognize copper as a source of Arizona's mineral wealth and create a unique look. Many artistic scenes of Arizona life depict the spirit and progress of the new state. The silver service was housed in a glass and wood display cabinet on the ship.

Following remodeling in 1929, the USS *Arizona* was the Navy's most modern battleship and became a powerful weapon of the Pacific Fleet. When the *Arizona* was sunk by the Japanese bombing of Pearl Harbor on 7 December 1941, many believed that the silver service had been lost as well, particularly after a piece of the admiral's own silver was salvaged and mistaken for the ship's service. But fortunately the service had been removed in January 1941, when the Navy, aware of the threat of war in the Pacific, stored the USS *Arizona* silver in Bremerton, Washington, before the ship left for Pearl Harbor.

In 1947 the silver was put on the USS *Tucson,* and following its decommission, on the USS *Adirondack* for a tour of active duty in the Mediterranean. Through a special loan agreement with the Navy, Governor Howard Pyle arranged for the silver to be exhibited at the state fair from 1953 to 1955. Arizona residents began to feel the silver should be returned "home" for public display rather than placed on a naval ship. In 1976 Mrs. Raul H. Castro, first lady of Arizona, successfully obtained its transfer to the state capitol building and today the entire silver service collection is exhibited in the Arizona State Capitol Museum in Phoenix.

Sterling was replacing plated ware in more homes, and by 1904 sterling had become the largest selling line for the company. In 1905 Reed & Barton's *Hepplewhite* pattern received an enthusiastic public response and was considered a significant achievement in the field of sterling flatware.

Dowse built upon the interests of Reed and Brabrook in furthering the impor-

London silverplated flatware, first produced in 1936, continues as a popular pattern for hotel ware. Featured on the cover of the Reed & Barton Food Service Division catalogue, 1998.

tance of design. The company had previously employed craftsmen as designers for the creation of new products. Dowse introduced the first design professionals with the hire of George Turner from the Rhode Island School of Design and August Miller from Tiffany's, both of whom served the company into the 1940s.

The French Renaissance was a strong influence in the first decade of the twentieth century, and Reed & Barton commissioned Ernest Meyers, a French artist and authority on the Renaissance period, and Max Boewe, a German die-cutter, to create a sterling pattern. *Francis I,* introduced in 1908 and named after the sixteenth-century Renaissance king, is an example of spectacular design, featuring fifteen different fruit groupings. It has since become the company's signature pattern and most enduring design.

In 1924 the Maharajah of Barwani in East India called for proposals to design a sterling silver dinner service. Reed & Barton submitted the award-winning design with their *Francis I* pattern and received the million-dollar award. Once it was completed, getting the dinner service there presented the larger challenge. Carefully packed in many small boxes, the order was shipped out of Taunton to New York, then to Liverpool and Bombay where it traveled 800 miles inland by train, 400 miles by mules, and the final 100 miles on the backs of the Maharajah's carriers.

The Fairmont Hotel in San Francisco has used Reed & Barton silver since its doors opened in 1907. Founder of the hotel, Ben Swig from Taunton sold newspapers as a boy outside the main gate of the Reed & Barton factory and throughout his life had a loyalty to the company. Circa 1974. Reed & Barton archives.

The decade of the 1920s was a period of general prosperity; people traveled more and this was reflected in an increase in sales in hotel ware. The Brown Palace in Denver; the Fairmont Hotel and the Mark Hopkins Hotel in San Francisco; the Capitol Hill Club in Washington, D.C.; dining rooms of the Grace Lines Ships; the Northern Pacific Railway, which was the first to provide dining car service to the Pacific Coast; Harvard University; and the Sheraton hotels were Reed & Barton customers. In Detroit, Michigan, salesman J. F. Dean used his bonus money to become a member of the Detroit Athletic Club and along the way managed to secure the club's silverware business. He also became a friend of a restaurant proprietor named Ellsworth M. Statler, who was planning a chain of hotels across the country.

Following World War I Americans looked for "a return to normalcy," away from involvement in European affairs, and an isolationist sentiment prevailed. It was a time of renewed interest in Americana that included the popularity of colonial pewter reflected in reproduction work at Reed & Barton.

At the turn of the century, the jeweler was the premiere distributor of silverware, observes Sinclair Weeks Jr. "Up until the 1920s, the jeweler had such a

1620-1970
LANDING OF THE
PILGRIMS AT PLYMOUTH
21 DECEMBER 1620
THE MAYFLOWER
IN WHOSE CABIN WAS SIGNED
THE COMPACT IN
CAPE COD HARBOR
21 NOV 1620

THE ROOSEVELT CUP

To commemorate the 350th anniversary of the landing of the Pilgrims in 1620, the National Association of Congregational Christian Churches commissioned Reed & Barton to produce a limited number of medallions in sterling silver and Britannia metal in 1970. A special presentation of the medals was made to President Richard Nixon. Reed & Barton archives.

The Professional Polo Association held the first "Corrigan's Cup" polo match in Dallas, Texas, in August 1984, with First Lady Nancy Reagan presenting the cup to the winning team to toast victory. The trophy contained 217 troy ounces of silver. Reed & Barton was selected by Corrigan's Jewelers of Texas to create the cup because of their extensive experience in the design and creation of precious metal trophies. 1984. Reed & Barton archives.

The Roosevelt Cup, shown in the 1910 trophy catalogue. Selected from competing designs by Theodore Roosevelt for the Jamestown Fair Yacht Races. Nineteen seven marked the 300th anniversary of the founding of the Jamestown Colony. Reed & Barton archives.

hold on the business that he could put his own mark on the product. For example, we have made silverware for many years for Shreve's in Boston. On old Shreve services, it is not marked Reed & Barton, but Shreve, Crump & Low. In the 1920s the silver companies through advertising developed their own brand identity. In the industry we have built our brand names, a development of great importance."

The Sterling Silver Manufacturers Association was formed in 1919 to place more emphasis on style and price than competing on retail terms. The silver manufacturers looked to increase sales through group advertising and in 1926 changed their name to the Sterling Silversmiths Guild of America. When standard practices applied to all dealers, it reduced the individual jeweler's ability to shop for a better deal. Reed & Barton President Sinclair Weeks, who participated in the group's formation and served in its leadership, looked to the collaborative effort of the Guild to deal with the excess of competition and the destructiveness of price cutting by establishing standard practices. It was a position that the successive presidencies of his son-in-law Roger Hallowell and son Sinclair Weeks Jr. would have an increasingly difficult time maintaining within the Guild.

In 1928 Reed & Barton purchased the company of Dominick & Haff of Newark, New Jersey, with an interest in increasing the volume of sterling sales. The two companies shared many similarities. Dominick & Haff, founded in 1821, had an old and respected name in the industry, with a line of high quality sterling flatware and holloware, and a similar source of distribution through fine retail jewelry and silverware stores. Retailers easily accepted the merger of the two lines of products under the Reed & Barton name. The acquisition changed Reed & Barton's focus from a balance of nickel silver, white metal, and sterling to a predominantly sterling oriented firm. The shift from plated to sterling silver also represented a shift in the company's business from hotel to retail sales.

The Great Crash in 1929 found Reed & Barton so overextended, because of the heavy volume of business during the last few months of 1928, that they could not deliver their orders on time. The company compensated the following year to meet the anticipated demand for the busy season and borrowed heavily to finance operations to create a good inventory by October. With the stock market crash that month, sales plummeted; retailers canceled orders and began returning merchandise to the factory. For the consumer faced with a choice of necessities, silver was always a postponable purchase.

Display of sterling flatware includes patterns, *above left to right*: *Pointed Antique, American Federal, Spanish Baroque, Tara, Burgundy, English Provincial, Grande Renaissance, Hampton Court; below left to right*: *Francis I, Golden Ashmont, Ashmont, 18th Century, Woodwind, English Chippendale.* 1994. Reed & Barton archives.

As president of the company, Sinclair Weeks made gradual reductions in staff and applied rigid cost cutting throughout the factory. The company made its own writing pads from waste paper and out-of-date price lists. The concern for Weeks was to keep as many employed as possible and the company going. "I don't care whether I make any money, just give us enough business so we can keep them going." Every effort was made to develop new business and keep the work force busy. Even a new flatware pattern was introduced, *Marlborough,* adapted from an 1898 Reed & Barton design. It sold on a break-even basis, with sterling silver spoons selling for seventy-five cents each while the metal alone cost the company thirty-five cents.

President Ronald Reagan and Nancy Reagan, as guests of honor at the 250th anniversary of the birth of George Washington, were presented with replicas of a taperstick that belonged to Nelly Custis Lewis, the granddaughter of George Washington. John Gilroy, head of the Design Department, went to Mt. Vernon, measured the original silver piece, and made a working drawing for the team of Reed & Barton craftsmen to reproduce. 1982. Photograph reproduced courtesy of the Mount Vernon Ladies' Association, Mount Vernon, Virginia.

The hotel business was in decline within the central cities, and Reed & Barton's shift to sterling actually cushioned the company from the most severe impact of the depression. The excellent machine tool quality and equipment from Dominick & Haff's Newark plant was brought to Taunton and improved Reed & Barton's production capacity. A Dominick & Haff pattern, *Pointed Antique* was an old, popular design that appealed to traditional purchasers of sterling, especially in the Northeast, the geographic region that dominated sales at the time with New York the leader. *Pointed Antique,* derived from classic American colonial patterns such as those of Paul Revere, continued as an enduring seller and was presented at commemorative occasions. When President John F. Kennedy cut his inaugural cake in 1961, it was with a *Pointed Antique* cake knife. In 1965 a new carrier, the USS *America,* was launched and carried a sterling holloware silver service made by Reed & Barton in the *Pointed Antique* design.

The experience of the depression left a cautious approach to finance and sales at Reed & Barton that stayed with the company into the post World War II years as others in the industry were more venturesome in charting new areas, such as the growth of stainless steel.

A competitive silverware industry, characterized by aggressive sales campaigns and the courting of consumer demand, was a part of the new century. Reflected in the language were newly introduced business phrases such as "market appeal" and "buying motives." The expansion of marketing and advertising assisted but never diminished the importance of the individual salesman on whom the volume of incoming orders depended. Conservative in nature, the keynote of company policy remained as it was in Henry Reed's day, "better metal," reflected in the quality of the product and an appreciation of its craftsmanship.

FOR THE DURATION: ONE BATTLE, ONE FRONT

Inspection of holloware pieces for the war effort. By V-J Day, Reed & Barton had provided more than three-quarters of all the silver holloware used by the Navy. Women played a much-needed role in the factory work force. Reed & Barton archives.

THE IMPACT OF a nation mobilizing for war was immediately felt at home. World War II would be destructive and far-reaching, affecting both soldier and civilian. America had resisted entering the war and was poorly prepared for combat. But when the Japanese launched their devastating surprise attack on Pearl Harbor in the early morning of 7 December 1941, Americans viewed the war as a highly principled, moral defense of the values and freedom of civilization. There was a sense of purpose and pride, of being connected to something larger and meaningful, of living and working with a special intensity to get the job done.

Lives would be uprooted, irrevocably changed, and a war so all encompassing became a mark of time to which events are placed, a watershed passing for this century. There would be no going back to a prewar America. In the demands of maintaining a technology-based army came the creation of new materials and means of production. The requirement of new skills for jobs that released the nation from the grip of a decade of depression produced a more equitable distribution of wealth and the rise of the middle class.

Support from the homefront was essential if the war was to be won. At Reed & Barton they knew victory belonged to those nations with the greater number of factories and the more efficient industrial workers. They knew in this total war the "soldier of the production line" was fighting alongside his brother in uniform. It would be a major conversion for a 117-year-old company devoted to the silversmith as craftsman producing products of art and beauty. This war for the first time in the company's history would determine the types of products made.

Severe restrictions were imposed on the use of certain metals for civilian production. With the company only able to supply six-piece place settings in a few sterling flatware patterns, the manufacture of sterling holloware and most sterling flatware was out for the duration. Silver, tin, copper, and nickel, essential to the production of high-quality plate, were no longer available for civilian output. But the armed forces needed forks and spoons, and the Navy with its expanded fleet required holloware.

While Vice President of Sales Joseph Martin worked to maintain good relations with the civilian customer base, the Reed & Barton sales force were ingenious in their outreach to obtain contracts for the manufacture of surgical instruments for the Army Medical Corps and the production of over 100,000 lifesaving radar "corner reflectors" for M.I.T. The company's staff, under the leadership of Colonel Arthur Ashworth and Plant Superintendent Arthur Schutzmeister, reorganized the factory for war work that required mass production techniques and new tooling, dies, and machinery. Equipment that could only be used for silverware production was placed in storage, and production in departments such as white metal rolling, chasing, and sterling flatware was suspended.

The work force increased, sizably augmented as elsewhere in the nation by women, and "Rosie the Riveter" was well represented in the Reed & Barton factory. In tribute to their contribution, the company management proudly acknowledged that "without them we could never have achieved such an outstanding production record."

The outstanding production record of the company was proudly credited to the increased number of women in the company's labor force. Reed & Barton archives.

Soldiers of the Production Line

Product specifications were formulated in detail by the Army and Navy and precisely followed. Inspectors from the branches of the armed services were a familiar presence in the factory.

Established U.S. Navy tradition required silver holloware aboard battleships and cruisers, which during peacetime were used in missions to foreign ports and for the entertainment of dignitaries. The admirals of the U.S. Navy's Great White Fleet of 1907, employing the first modern steel-armored battleships to circumnavigate the globe, were the official representatives of President Theodore Roosevelt for entertaining foreign kings and ministers. Reed & Barton became a major supplier of the Navy's silverware. By V-J Day, Reed & Barton had provided more than three-quarters of all the silver holloware used by the Navy. While in peacetime the company might be asked to make a few hundred silverplated water pitchers in a year, the demands of war increased this to 28,000.

It was the sheer volume of war production required amidst the urgency of delivery schedules, the scarcity of materials, and the drafting of so many experienced craftsmen that made the effort so formidable. Reed & Barton could take special pride that at the end of the war not a single piece of the company's production for the Navy was returned as being defective. This perfect record contributed to Reed & Barton's receiving the Army-Navy "E" award for excellence on 19 November 1943 with praise from the men of the fleet. "For in every ship in which they serve is the product of your hands. . . ."

Early in the war, nickel silver, carbon steel, and copper alloy were used as a base metal for plating. Nickel silver contains no silver but is a silvery-like metal that is an alloy of 18 percent nickel, 70 percent copper, and 12 percent zinc. At the end of 1942 when copper became unavailable and the nickel silver supply was shut off, the government selected Reed & Barton as a pilot plant for the development of a method of plating silver directly on steel. Reed & Barton successfully pioneered the development, receiving a letter of appreciation from the War Metallurgy Committee of the National Research Council.

During World War II Reed & Barton produced about a million pieces of silverplated holloware, an astonishing feat for a craft that did not readily lend itself to mass manufacturing techniques. But, as with the development of an engraving machine capable of cutting the required naval insignia on several dozen pieces simultaneously, the introduction of many new techniques led to greater speed in production and increased productivity per worker.

To save time in manufacturing and reduce government costs, Reed & Barton successfully persuaded the Navy to relax tradition and change the basic design specifications for its silverware. All applied mounts were eliminated, design was simplified and standardized, and distinguishing insignia of rank eliminated so that the same item could be used interchangeably in the war room or on the admiral's table. As a result, production increased significantly, and the company was turning out thousands of pieces for the Navy weekly for United States ships operating on all the seven seas.

★

Surgical Instruments by Reed & Barton

★

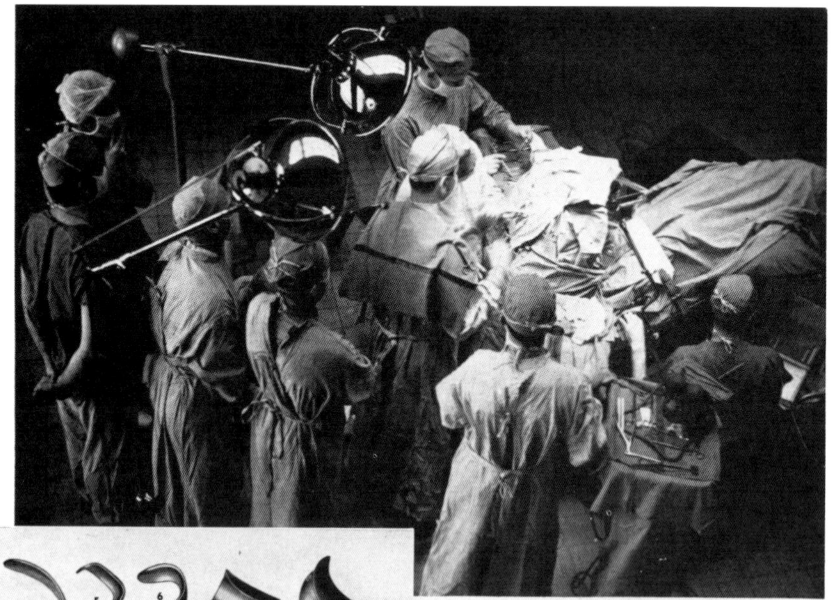

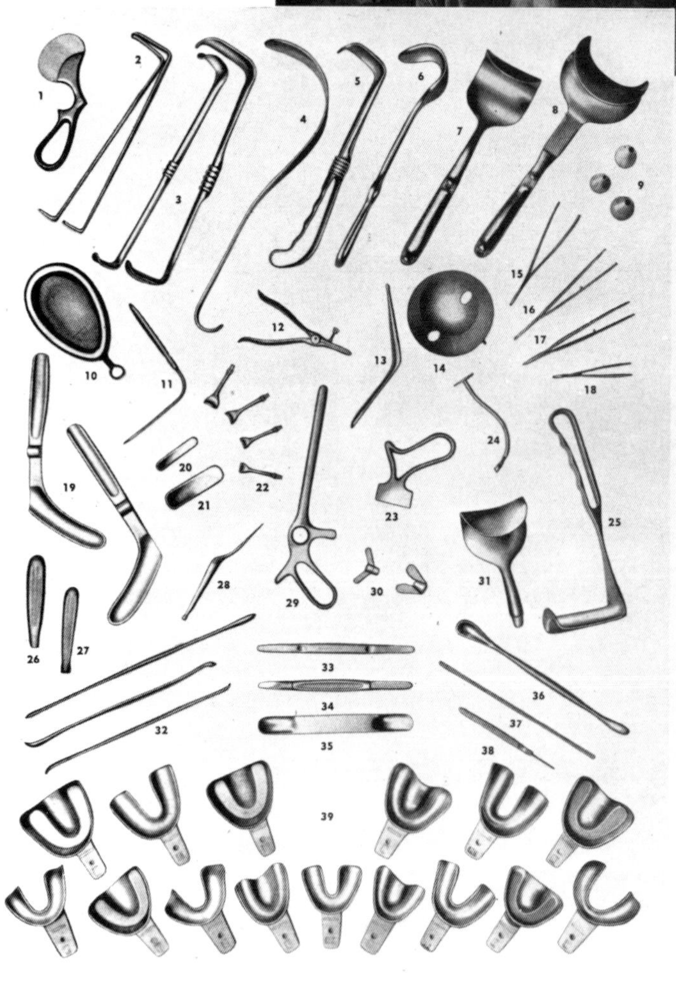

1—Plaster of Paris Saw
2—Tissue Retractors
3—Richardson-Eastman's Retractors
4—Deaver's Abdominal Retractor
5—Kelly's Abdominal Retractor
6—Fritch's Abdominal Retractor
7—Mayo's Abdominal Retractor
8—Doyen's Abdominal Retractor
9—Brown's Ear Specula
10—Anaesthesia Mask
11—Tongue Depressor
12—Nasal Speculum
13—Lithotomy Gorget
14—Head Light Reflector
15—Kelly's Tissue-Forceps
16—Mouse Tooth Tip Forceps
17—Dressing Forceps
18—Mayo's Tissue Forceps
19—Pratt's Rectal Speculum *
20—Anal Retractor *
21—Ives' Rectal Speculum *
22—Eye Retractors *
23—Bone Saw *
24—Breathing Tube
25—Abdominal Retractor *
26, 27—Mastoid Curette Handles
28—Teale's Gorget *
29—Satterlee's Saw *
30—Wing Nuts *
31—Mayo's Retractor *
32—Gall Bladder Scoops
33—Periosteal Elevator (*Navy Style*)
34—Periosteal Elevator (*Army Style*)
35—Brain Spatula
36—Gall Stone Scoop
37—Bullet Probe
38—Eye Spud
39—Dental Trays

*Casting

Flatware for the Troops

To feed the more than twelve million men and women in uniform required tens of millions of utensils, and for many years Reed & Barton had been supplying an important part of the Navy's peacetime flatware. There was justified satisfaction that none of the wartime flatware produced by Reed & Barton was ever rejected.

With the introduction of stainless steel, no silver coating was needed and the entire production of Army and Navy flatware shifted to stainless. A complete overhaul of the flatware manufacturing process was required. Dies were constructed differently because the toughness of the metal would break ordinary dies, and harsher polishing abrasives, such as emery, were introduced. Reed & Barton adapted and succeeded in manufacturing 100,000 stainless steel pieces a week, which was increased by the armed forces to 180,000 weekly and then to an incredible 210,000 forks and spoons per week. Such requirements spurred new economies and efficiencies of production.

By V-J Day, the company had produced over twenty-nine million forks and spoons, which, if laid end to end, would form a continuous line 3,300 miles long, or more than the distance from Taunton, Massachusetts, to Taunton, England.

The Surgical Instruments Division

A critical need existed for the production of surgical instruments that required adapting to working with steel, cast bronze, and chromium. Shortly after Pearl Harbor came the first request for the company to make a thousand nasal specula out of corrosion resisting steel. Though nasal specula had never been made by the surgical instruments industry in lots of more than a hundred at a time, Reed & Barton succeeded in making over 40,000 pieces, an accomplishment that demonstrated exceptional flexibility and adaptability. Matt Bury remembers the company working on a request for tin impression plates for dental work.

It was difficult finding sources from which to obtain the necessary metals that the company had never used before, sorting through a maze of procurement forms and government paper work, and adjusting to demanding delivery schedules. New metals required dies with the strength to form stainless steel, grinding compounds strong enough to polish the surface of steel, and welding techniques to replace soldering. When America's crude rubber supply was abruptly cut off

Display of surgical instruments made by Reed & Barton during the war. Reed & Barton archives.

★ ★ ★ ★ ★

THE RADAR CORNER REFLECTOR for life rafts was indeed an unusual product for a silverware factory to make. 1, the reflector all set up, ready for use; 2, the water proof package, less than two feet long, into which the entire reflector was telescoped; 3, life raft occupant removing the reflector from the package; 4, setting it up; 5, all set up, the reflector mast is attached to the life raft. Reproduced below (6) is a letter from a soldier whose life was saved by this ingenious device. (An excerpt from this letter is printed on the opposite page.)

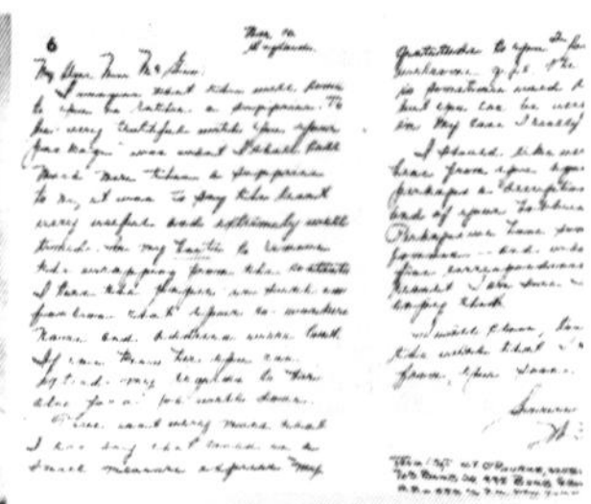

The introduction of radar during World War II made it possible to locate enemy targets; and the production of the corner reflector, a top-secret project by Reed & Barton in concert with M.I.T., helped save lives. Reed & Barton archives.

by Japanese conquests in the East Indies, Reed & Barton used sterling silver instead of hard rubber to manufacture breathing tubes, producing 45,000 of them in silver. And when the supply of copper became scarce, hundreds of thousands of bullet probes were similarly made from sterling silver.

Extreme care was necessary in the manufacture of surgical instruments to ensure that every surface had a smooth mirror finish. No corners, pits, or scratches that might harbor disease-bearing bacteria could be tolerated, nor sharp or rough edges that could bruise delicate tissue. There would be no unnecessary casualties on the operating table if the production soldiers of Reed & Barton could prevent them!

During World War II Reed & Barton produced close to one million diverse surgical instruments, which were sent to medical stations and outposts throughout the world. They were packed in special cases lined with moisture-proof paper as protection against variations in climate. Two weeks after V-J Day ended the war on 12 August 1945, the Army Medical Purchasing Office wrote to the company in appreciation. "We of the Medical Department fully realize what an important part your firm played in the development, production, and delivery of supplies so vitally needed for the preservation of the lives of our gifted men and women. We wish to take this opportunity to thank your organization for the splendid cooperation and untiring efforts which helped so materially to make the Medical Department's record in this war so outstanding."

Radar to the Rescue

When flying ace Eddie Rickenbacker crash-landed in the Pacific in 1942, it was only miraculous luck that he was spotted after twenty-two days, drifting in his life raft barely visible in the vast ocean expanse. Most aviators were unable to be spotted by a plane flying overhead and were lost at sea. Scientists who formerly worked in laboratory isolation were now enlisted in the national effort as problem solvers for the nation's military and government leadership. The introduction of radar made it possible to locate enemy targets even under heavy overcast conditions and for battleships to fire accurately at night. With the invention of the corner reflector by scientists of the National Defense Research Committee, developed from a model designed at the Radiation Laboratories of M.I.T., radar

As Lovely As Tomorrow.....
FRANCIS FIRST
POINTED ANTIQUE
GEORGIAN ROSE
GUILDHALL
FRAGRANCE
FRENCH RENAISSANCE
YOUR REED & BARTON Solid Silver
Each of the appointments for gracious living you choose today helps your home of tomorrow come true. And one of your most important purchases at this time should be the Reed & Barton Solid Silver that will parallel the pattern of your married life.
War means that silver manufacture is confined to the most commonly used pieces, such as knives, forks, spoons and butter spreaders . . . which are available today. But remember that when war is over, you can complete your service and add all those pieces which are temporarily unobtainable. Meanwhile . . . treasure the Reed & Barton Solid Silver you buy now as the most valued possession of your hope chest . . . for tomorrow.
SEND FOR THIS HELPFUL HOSTESS BOOK
Reed & Barton
STERLING SILVER
IN PEACE, FOSTERING A HIGH STANDARD OF GRACIOUS LIVING
. . . TODAY, DEFENDING THAT STANDARD BY WAR PRODUCTION
REED & BARTON
Box 990, Taunton, Mass.
☐ Please send illustrated literature on pattern named in margin.
☐ Enclosed is 10c for 64-page booklet, "How To Be A Successful Hostess" full of entertainment tips and advice on selection, care and use of Sterling Silver.
Name
Address
JIM-A-43

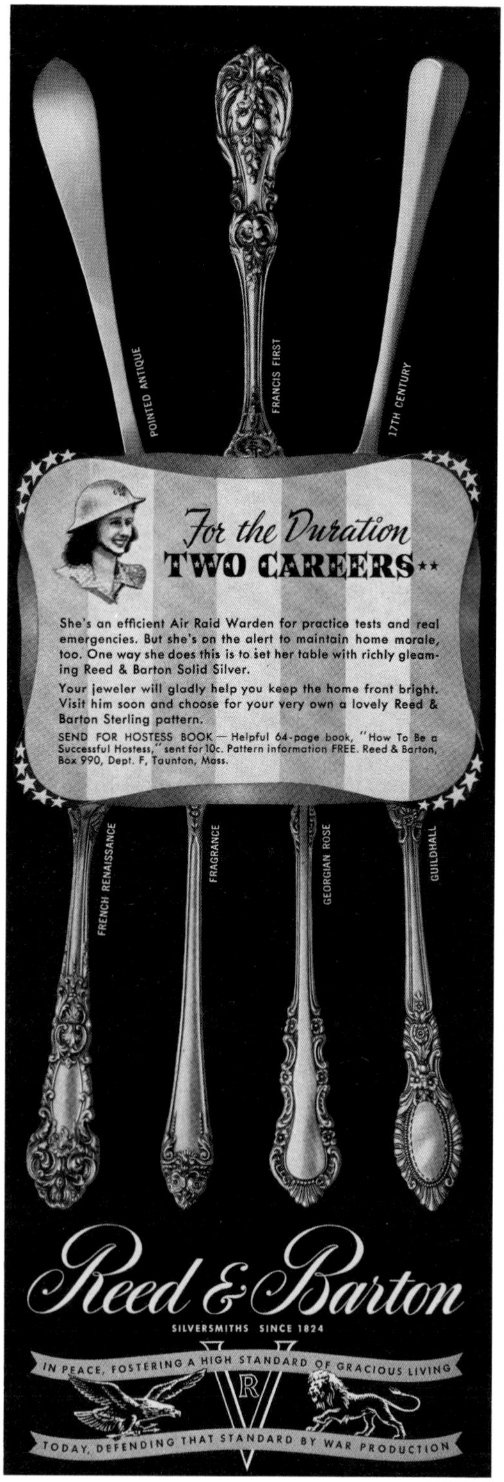
POINTED ANTIQUE
FRANCIS FIRST
17TH CENTURY
For the Duration
TWO CAREERS**
She's an efficient Air Raid Warden for practice tests and real emergencies. But she's on the alert to maintain home morale, too. One way she does this is to set her table with richly gleaming Reed & Barton Solid Silver.
Your jeweler will gladly help you keep the home front bright. Visit him soon and choose for your very own a lovely Reed & Barton Sterling pattern.
SEND FOR HOSTESS BOOK — Helpful 64-page book, "How To Be a Successful Hostess," sent for 10c. Pattern information FREE. Reed & Barton, Box 990, Dept. F, Taunton, Mass.
FRENCH RENAISSANCE
FRAGRANCE
GEORGIAN ROSE
GUILDHALL
Reed & Barton
SILVERSMITHS SINCE 1824
IN PEACE, FOSTERING A HIGH STANDARD OF GRACIOUS LIVING
TODAY, DEFENDING THAT STANDARD BY WAR PRODUCTION

While wartime production of silver for civilian use was severely curtailed, advertisements looked to the peacetime resumption of silver purchases and the broadened market appeal of sterling from the carriage trade to the growing middle class. Reed & Barton archives.

waves could be bounced back from the searching plane to identify the raft's position and rescue the aviator.

The corner reflector consisted of eleven triangles of fine wire mesh mounted on a collapsible metal framework, which was folded and packed into a waterproof carton less than two feet long and two inches square. With the instrument assembled and mounted on its three-foot mast, radar beams from every direction would bounce back from its numerous surfaces the way light is reflected from the faces of a diamond. The project was surrounded by strict secrecy and given the name "Phyllis."

Reed & Barton produced the first experimental lot of 1,000 reflectors and perfected the first practical working models towards providing the necessary volume required. An effective partnership was established between Reed & Barton, the scientists and technicians of M.I.T., and the research group engaged in developing the corner reflector. All became regular visitors to Taunton involved in the design of new machine tools and new processes of manufacture. The radar reflectors became standard equipment for all military and naval planes engaged in over-water flight. With patriotic determination Reed & Barton produced over 100,000 assembled corner reflectors by the end of the war.

The reply of one recipient personalizes the lifesaving impact of the corner reflector. When packing one of the reflectors to be used by Army fliers engaged in bombing Germany from British bases on the other side of the North Sea, two Reed & Barton girls included their names and addresses and received an appreciative letter of response. "There isn't very much that I can say that could in small measure express my gratitude to you for your most welcome gift. The word 'Thanks' is sometimes used rather loosely. But you can be sure that in my case I really mean it. . . ."

The Reed & Barton staff soon learned that change was the rule, and it seemed as soon as they mastered the manufacture of one type of model, it was replaced by another. They also realized that their own experience could contribute to the way scientific instruments were manufactured and found that making an antenna wave guide required as much craftsmanship as the most expensive sterling silver tea set. All radar units contained the three principal components of a transmitter, the antenna wave guide or nozzle, and the antenna itself. All the parts of the wave guide assembly were produced at Reed & Barton, silver soldered to the main tube and plated with precious metals, some in silver, some in

Reed & Barton workers proudly march through Taunton to ceremonies for the Army-Navy production award for excellence. Reed & Barton archives.

gold. The wave guide, though an intricate mechanism, was essentially a bent copper tube several feet long and rectangular in cross-section. One of the problems in the manufacture of the wave guides was bending the rectangular tubes which would wrinkle and distort on the sides. Reed & Barton was able to correct this by filling the tube with "pitch," the way hand chasers did when preparing to decorate a piece of fine silverware, using a large hydraulic press to squeeze the tube gently into shape on a pair of steel-faced hardwood dies. There was difficulty, as well, plating and finishing the interior surfaces of the tubes which were silverplated and had to be polished to a mirror smoothness to enable the radar waves to pass through them properly.

The introduction of *The Silver Lining*, a newsletter to keep in touch with servicemen from the factory, was so well received that it expanded to become a newsletter for the company. Reed & Barton archives.

All Out for Victory

Everyone was working for the same objective, to end the war and bring the boys back home. The Reed & Barton factory had been converted into a war plant with shifts around the clock. Reed & Barton had their own Air Raid Precautions Committee to provide warning and protection against enemy air raids.

Members of the sales department assumed extra war-related responsibilities. Matthew Bury took over the flatware contracts, assisted the time study department, ran the employees' suggestion system, and after work as a member of the Coast Guard Reserve, joined other civilians on evening shore patrol. Some jobs required total personal conversion. When war eliminated his work with sterling holloware, master silversmith Albert Dumoulin applied his talents to the surgical instruments division and secret radar projects.

It was "all out for victory" on the job and after hours. The use of blood plasma to treat the wounded was a new medical advancement and many Reed & Barton employees donated to the Red Cross Mobile Blood Donor Unit, with women serving as Red Cross nurses. There was active participation in civil defense organizations and the local Community Chest War Fund that Joseph Martin chaired while William Hurley applied his public relations skills by handling publicity for the Taunton Red Cross in their fund raising campaigns.

From Factory to Front Line: *The Silver Lining* Kept in Touch

It was the idea of Reed & Barton president Sinclair Weeks that servicemen from the company would welcome hearing from the factory in a newsletter, and in March 1942 a one-page mimeographed letter was sent to the then 33 soldiers, sailors, and marines. The number of servicemen from Reed & Barton eventually numbered 385, five of whom did not live to return to the postwar America they had fought for, but who were remembered with their colleagues in the company's published tribute, *Marching Together.*

The coveted newsletter sent monthly increased to forty pages and was called *The Silver Lining.* The publication was totally written by employees with every department in the company represented. The "Correspondence Exchange" drew letters from Reed & Barton servicemen stationed throughout the world.

Within the "Correspondence Exchange" of the 30 April 1943 issue, excerpts from the many letters received include moving references to the company and *The Silver Lining.*

> Needless to say, *The Silver Lining* is one of the most enjoyable pieces of news that I receive each month. It's like being right in the Shop with the gang again. . . . I am in what was once Battery F from Taunton. It is still mostly made up of Taunton boys, and they enjoy all the articles in *The Silver Lining* as much as I do. They like the bits of poetry that appear in each issue, and say: 'Give us more!' . . .
>
> –Howard Manchester, Camp Cooke, Cal.
> (Plating Room)

> I just received your swell gifts. . . . I cannot express my gratitude too freely. . . . My joy is in my heart, and my buddies know it. They all say R&B must be a swell organization to work for. I hope all is going according to plan at the shop. It would be swell to visit R&B again, for just a little while at least. . . .
>
> –Walter Gwozdz, Overseas
> (Hotel Department)

> The old shop appears to be running smoothly. You've got to hand it to those girls. I never thought they'd be taking over some of those large presses. . . .
>
> –Roland Dion, Newport, R.I.
> (Stamp Room)

> *The Silver Lining* along with the daily *Gazette,* give a fellow many an enjoyable evening. I show *The Silver Lining* to my buddies, and their opinion of the set-up

you people are doing for our behalf is highly recommended. Mighty few concerns have taken so much interest in their previous employees. I'm very grateful to be connected with the R&B enterprise. . . .

–John Goldonowicz, Ft. Bliss, Texas
(Plating Room)

At my first meal, much to my surprise I saw some silverware before me which looked rather familiar. Sure enough it was by R&B. It was just about a month before that I had helped make it. . . .

–Edmund Gurdak, Middletown, Conn.
(Flatware Polishing Department)

Don't forget me when you are mailing *The Silver Lining*. . . . I've been moving around a great deal. I've been up to the front again. . . . I had some close calls. I hope this North Africa campaign comes to a close soon. Watch the newspapers . . . as you read, well, some place in that good news I'm playing the game. . . .

–Raymond Strojny, Overseas
(Flatware Polishing Department)

Reed and Barton is certainly doing a wonderful job of keeping her boys in the service well informed of what is happening about the shop. . . . How is my grandfather Bert Robinson? Tell him and Mr. Pepper I was asking for them. I sure wish I were back working side by side with them.

–Wendell Robinson, Camp Hulen, Texas
(Hotel Department)

The newsletter proved so popular throughout the company that *The Silver Lining* became a company publication for employees in April 1946.

In Recognition: The Army-Navy Production Award for Excellence

It was industry's most prestigious award–the Army-Navy "E" for excellence–the esteemed "E" flag. Only 5 percent of the nation's factories received the honor. Wearing their sterling pins, Reed & Barton employees marched proudly in an "E" parade through the streets of Taunton. When Admiral Cluverius presented

The coveted "E" flag is held at the company ceremony award on 19 November 1943. President Sinclair Weeks and General Manager Arthur Ashworth to his right, who succeeded him as president, are pictured in the center. Qualification for the award had to be renewed every six months, and Reed & Barton succeeded in earning it four times until the war ended. Reed & Barton archives.

Reed & Barton with the "E" flag in a ceremony held at the company on 19 November 1943, he said, "You who previously made the most beautifully finished silver in the world, are now producing those things that pertain to the physical welfare of the men in the armed forces. You have met this call." General Manager Arthur Ashworth replied, "Gone are the days when someone said, 'It can't be done!' Who says it can't be done? You have done it! . . . Our workers just wanted to do their part to back up the boys on the front line."

The award had to be renewed every six months by the addition of a star to the flag, and by the war's end Reed & Barton had received four such stars of excellence. To the normally taciturn, somber Ashworth, who had served as a colonel in World War I, the achievement was a dramatic moment that tapped a well of feeling and remained for him the company's finest hour.

For those at Reed & Barton during this period of time, there was an intense feeling of pride and sense of being connected to the national effort. World War II was a total war requiring total commitment, and everyone became accustomed to taking on the unaccustomed, for the duration.

A CALL TO THE CABINET

THE DECADE of the 1950s is remembered as a banner time for sterling silver sales, a productive period for Reed & Barton, and a partnership between the presidency of Dwight D. Eisenhower and the nation's business community. Sinclair Weeks, appointed as Secretary of Commerce in 1952, brought his years of experience in business and public service to a personal understanding of the needs of industry.

In his private journals Sinclair Weeks describes himself "by training, experience, and nature, a businessman in both manufacturing and banking. I agreed with President Coolidge who had earned wide attention by insisting, 'The chief business of America is business.' I wanted to go to Washington to foster, develop and promote decent private business by wise national government policies and programs. The defense of private enterprise and of sound business principles was my theme.

"The importance of industry and commerce to the people of Massachusetts was emphasized by the sight of our famous 'Sacred Cod,' hung since the colonial era beneath the Bullfinch golden dome of our Massachusetts State House. This five-foot reproduction is intended to keep our legislators aware of what business has done and can do for the public welfare. One of my life jobs has been to keep legislators from forgetting that duty."

In 1923 Sinclair Weeks was a banker with the First National Bank of Boston, when he became president of Reed & Barton. At the time he was pursuing the path of his father's business career combined with public service. His father, John Weeks, had a successful investment banking career as a co-founder and partner of the brokerage house of Hornblower & Weeks and the First National Bank of Boston.

Dedication of the Weeks Bridge in Cambridge, adjacent to Harvard University, in memory of the public service contributions of Secretary of War John Weeks. 1927. Photograph courtesy of Sinclair Weeks Jr.

The partnership of business and public service was evident in the careers of John Wingate Weeks and his son Sinclair Weeks.

John Wingate Weeks served as Secretary of War in the cabinet of President Calvin Coolidge. Cabinet meeting, *left to right*, head of the table: President Calvin Coolidge, Treasury Secretary Andrew W. Mellon, Attorney General John G. Sargent, Secretary of the Navy Curtis D. Wilbur, Secretary of Agriculture William M. Jardine, Secretary of Labor James John Davis. *Left to right*, bottom side of the table: Secretary of State Frank B. Kellogg, Secretary of War John Wingate Weeks, Postmaster General Harry S. New, Secretary of the Interior Hubert Work, Secretary of Commerce Herbert Clark Hoover. 1924. Photograph courtesy of Sinclair Weeks Jr. Photograph identification courtesy of Calvin Coolidge Memorial Foundation.

Now Sinclair Weeks was following the call of his father-in-law William B. H. Dowse to continue the family management at Reed & Barton. Weeks as C.E.O. brought to the company a personal, caring interest for the workers, enthusiastically presiding over numerous events of employee recognition and social functions. The Half-Century Club and Quarter-Century Club were formed to recognize those with long service to the company.

His son Sinclair Jr. remembers during World War II when Reed & Barton received "a rather substantial" order from the Navy for silverware to be used on a number of the ships. "It seemed to my father that spending money during a national emergency for sterling silverware for the fleet was a terrible waste of money and entirely unnecessary." Weeks contacted Secretary of the Navy Frank Knox and suggested that the order to his company be canceled, and it was. "My father was a life-long Republican, as was his father, and believed the least government is the best government. It's getting more and more difficult to follow this path."

In his beloved New England, Sinclair Weeks would point with pride to the three-pronged alliance of modern business progress: Research, Banking, and Manufacturing. Businessmen, he notes, "were quick to tap the 'think tanks' of our vast system of educational institutions" and willing to raise venture capital for ideas that "poured from our lecture halls and laboratories such as high voltage transmission, digital equipment, computer operated systems, and other

Sinclair Weeks served as Secretary of Commerce in the cabinet of President Dwight Eisenhower. Cabinet Meeting, 29 July 1955. *Left to right:* Wilton B. Persons, Deputy Assistant to the President; Henry Cabot Lodge, U.S. Representative to the United Nations; Douglas McKay, Secretary of the Interior; George M. Humphrey, Secretary of the Treasury; Richard M. Nixon, Vice President; Herbert Brownell, Attorney General; Sinclair Weeks, Secretary of Commerce; Oveta Culp Hobby, Secretary of Health, Education, and Welfare; Philip Young, Civil Service Commissioner; Rowland Hughes, Budget Director; Arthur S. Flemming, Director, Office of Defense Mobilization; Maxwell M. Rabb, Secretary of the Cabinet; James P. Mitchell, Secretary of Labor; Arthur E. Summerfield, Postmaster General; John Foster Dulles, Secretary of State; President Dwight D. Eisenhower; Charles E. Wilson, Secretary of Defense; Ezra Taft Benson, Secretary of Agriculture; Harold E. Stassen, Special Assistant to the President for Disarmament; Sherman Adams, Assistant to the President. Photograph courtesy of Sinclair Weeks Jr. Photograph identification courtesy of the Dwight D. Eisenhower Library.

modern technological wizardry. From the day of erecting the 'Sacred Cod' to the probing of the outermost reaches of space, the spirit of invention, capital investment, manufacturing, shipping and all such ingredients of job creation and tinkering for money have been ingrained with our people."

There were close social and political ties to other prominent New Englanders including Henry Cabot Lodge and Leverett Saltonstall. All three had graduated from Harvard and subsequently served as members of its Board of Overseers. Saltonstall and Sinclair Weeks were both citizens of Newton, where Weeks served as mayor. "Members of our three families since colonial times had been holding various positions of public, military and party trust. Cabot's grandfather, the Senior Henry Cabot Lodge, and my father, John Wingate Weeks, both were U.S. Senators from Massachusetts and were in office at the same time. My father was Secretary of War in the Harding and Coolidge cabinets. Lodge and I became members of the Eisenhower cabinet. Cabot's grandfather, Senior Senator Lodge, had nominated my father as the Republican candidate for President of the United States in 1916." When Cabot Lodge resigned his Senate seat on 4 February 1944 to serve in the war, Governor Saltonstall appointed Sinclair Weeks in his place.

Sinclair Weeks, an admirer of Herbert Hoover, escorts the former President and Commerce Secretary at a Commerce Department reception, 6 October 1954. Photograph courtesy of Sinclair Weeks Jr.

Weeks also had national responsibilities as Republican State Chairman, Republican State Finance Committee Chairman, Republican National Committee Member, Republican National Committee Treasurer, and Chairman, Republican National Finance Committee in 1952. Daughter Frances, married to Roger Hallowell, became a Republican National Committee Member and his son Bill, a Massachusetts State Senator.

The crowning achievement for Weeks was his leadership role in the initiation of the federal interstate highway system. Radio listeners on 29 June 1956 heard Washington announcer Richard Rendell describe the largest peacetime spending program ever to be undertaken. "In midmorning President Eisenhower signed into law the 33 billion dollar highway construction bill, and within minutes Secretary of Commerce Sinclair Weeks released 1.25 billion dollars to get the program underway."

"Engineers and political leaders of both parties for years had visualized some sort of highway links between states as necessary," writes Weeks in his journal. "But only sporadic roads were built without any over-all giant planning." It was an accomplishment requiring years of intense planning by Weeks, "presentations before stormy congressional hearings, government conferences, addressing business and labor organizations nation-wide, the general public and a co-

President Dwight Eisenhower with trophy awarded in his name to the winner of the National Celebrities Tournament, held at the Congressional Country Club in Washington, D.C. Reed & Barton was selected to make the Eisenhower trophy. 1954. Reed & Barton archives.

ordinated drive by press and government. America at last was about to move forward on seven-league boots. I'm glad I had the opportunity to play a real role in starting that historic journey."

Weeks was gratified when he read in President Eisenhower's book *Mandate for Change* his description of the interstate. "This great highway system will stand in part as a monument to the man in my Cabinet who headed the department responsible for it and who, himself, spent long hours mapping out the program and battling it through the Congress–Secretary of Commerce Sinclair Weeks."

During his tenure the St. Lawrence Seaway was opened. The range of department responsibilities for Weeks included such diverse areas as foreign commerce, aviation, weather, and census. The responsibility of the Census Bureau for collecting accurate information was dramatized by the "census clock," set up in the Commerce building lobby. It recorded the exact population of the United States as spectators watched its figures displayed on a revolving drum.

"It was to help Americans know their strength–especially their economic strength that our Department took many steps to improve its fact-finding and record-keeping agencies, including the Census Bureau. We not only increased the range of official figures but also the speed by which they were collected and distributed. This latter excellence was by the introduction of the high speed computer, which produced the 1960 census in record time.

"Just before I retired from office, the 'clock' registered at 11 A.M. October 16, 1958, exactly 175 million population. The first national count came when George Washington was president in 1790–four million. Enumerators rode horse-back and often were menaced by hostile Indians on the frontier."

But there were many other important statistics gathered, including those about economics and industry. New scientific and technological knowledge was being developed and new industries emerging with the creation of millions of jobs, observed Weeks. "As a manufacturer I had appreciated and often used science and technology in our own companies–in fact, we had commercial dealings with the Bureau. I had looked with keen interest on the 'necklace' of science-oriented industries that had sprung up along the Massachusetts Charles River and Route 128. I like to believe that many of the advanced technological ideas that today characterize our super-modern age came to birth in our research and development commerce agencies."

Of course you'll choose Sterling
FRANCIS FIRST
CLASSIC FASHION
Beyond a doubt you've dreamed of beautiful solid silver for your table . . . the enduring loveliness of an authentic Reed & Barton design. One of the many famous Reed & Barton patterns is destined to bring you years of special pride and pleasure, for the name Reed & Barton on sterling is your assurance of master craftsmanship and lasting satisfaction.
REED & BARTON
STERLING MADE BY ONE OF THE WORLD'S LEADING SILVERSMITHS — ESTABLISHED 1824
6-piece place settings approximately $24.50 to $33, including tax, at leading stores.
Helpful Hostess Hints: For fascinating booklet, "How To Be A Successful Hostess," send 10c to Box 990 LF, Taunton, Mass.
HEPPELWHITE
BURGUNDY
MARLBOROUGH

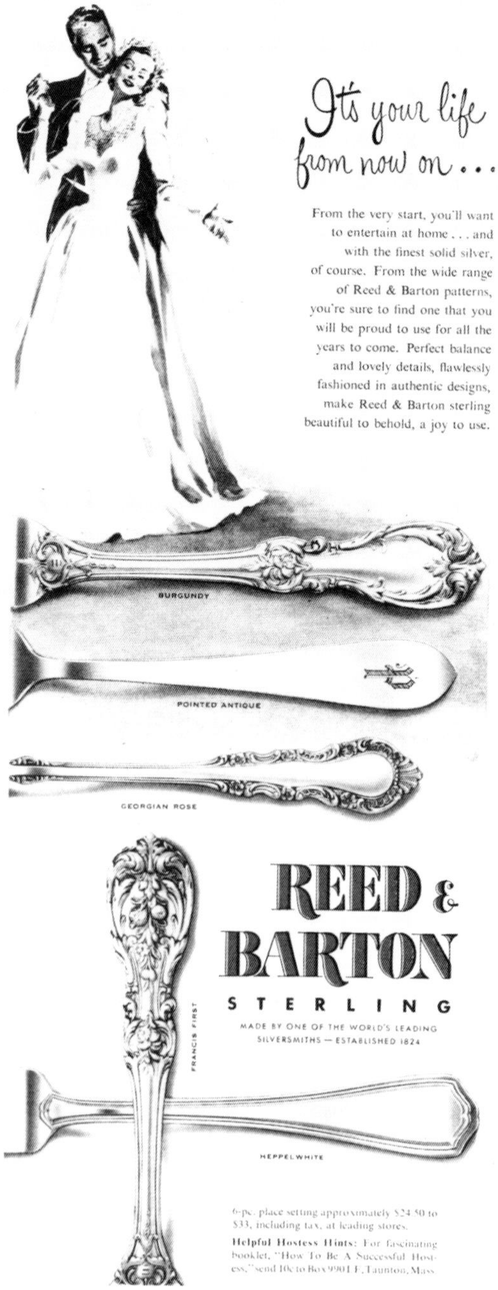
It's your life from now on . . .
From the very start, you'll want to entertain at home . . . and with the finest solid silver, of course. From the wide range of Reed & Barton patterns, you're sure to find one that you will be proud to use for all the years to come. Perfect balance and lovely details, flawlessly fashioned in authentic designs, make Reed & Barton sterling beautiful to behold, a joy to use.
BURGUNDY
POINTED ANTIQUE
GEORGIAN ROSE
REED & BARTON
STERLING
MADE BY ONE OF THE WORLD'S LEADING SILVERSMITHS — ESTABLISHED 1824
FRANCIS FIRST
HEPPELWHITE
6-pc. place setting approximately $24.50 to $33, including tax, at leading stores.
Helpful Hostess Hints: For fascinating booklet, "How To Be A Successful Hostess," send 10c to Box 990 LF, Taunton, Mass.

THE DECADE of the fifties and much of the sixties was a time when sterling shined for the silver industry and Reed & Barton. Sterling had broadened its market appeal from the carriage trade to the growing middle class following the end of World War II. Consumers had the savings and the desire to spend following the war, increased earnings, and a higher disposable income that made sterling more affordable. And sterling was "the real thing," a purchase that would be long lasting, a family heirloom, and the correct way of setting a table for dining, particularly for occasions of importance by the "successful hostess."

The nation's presidents entertained with sterling. President Harry Truman served guests aboard the presidential yacht *Williamsburg* with his set of *Francis I*, as did the Eisenhowers at their Gettysburg farm. The industry's sterling flatware sales rose eight-fold, from $6.6 million to $51 million, between 1938 and 1948. The increased volume of sterling flatware sales was stimulated by the stable cost of silver from 1946 through 1960. For the silver manufacturer each sterling teaspoon was worth about four silverplated ones in sales dollars and with a higher percentage markup was more profitable.

Advertisements featuring sterling patterns. Sterling became more popular to the growing middle class following World War II. The new consumers had the savings and the willingness to spend. *Life*, 1 May 1950; *Life*, 11 September 1950. Reed & Barton archives.

The potential industry volume was dependent on the number of brides who would be choosing a pattern, rather than the price of sterling, projected Bill Hurley, vice president of marketing. The future would be judged on the basis of demographics and marriage eligibility. That sterling silver was desirable to own was understood.

Reed & Barton employed market research studies extensively to survey the design preferences of young women who would soon be potential customers as homemakers. Based on this research, a pattern was then designed, tested for

Promotional contests with an opportunity to win sterling silver were both a popular way for the company to introduce new patterns, especially to young people as future consumers, and a marketing outreach of consumer preference during the 1950s and 1960s.

Right, Sterling silver contest introduces *Classic Rose* pattern in 1954. Reed & Barton archives.

Below, High school girls were the focus of this sterling silver contest. Photograph first appeared in the April 1961 edition of *Seventeen.* Reed & Barton archives.

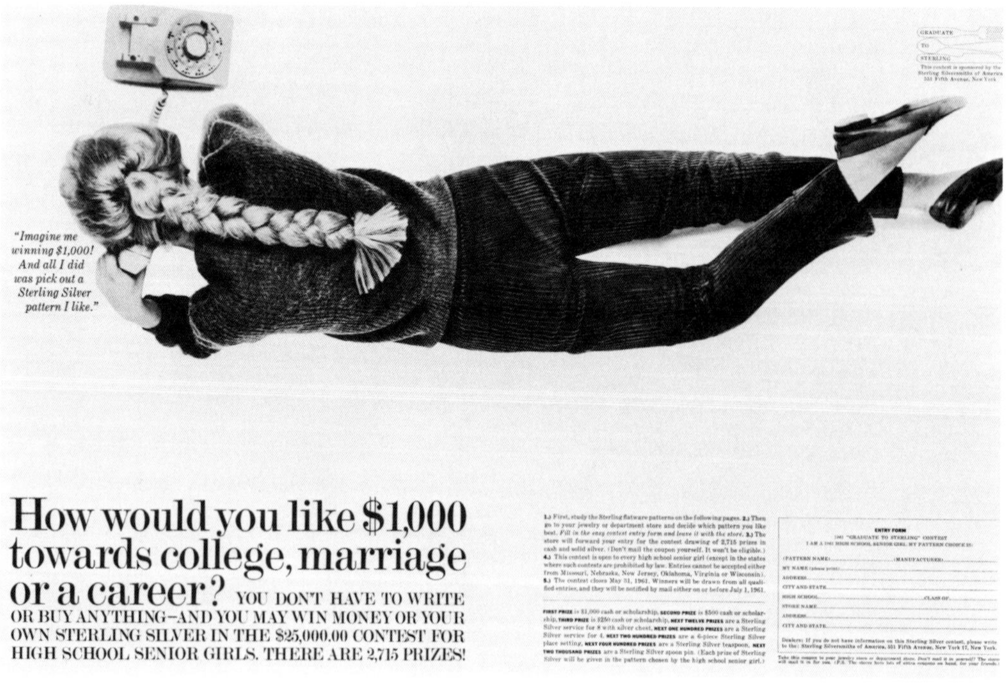

appeal, and heavily promoted. During the 1950s the company successfully integrated silver with fashion, so well that Reed & Barton's latest sterling flatware pattern appeared not only to be in step with lifestyle developments but in fact setting the pace. The introduction of Reed & Barton sterling flatware and accompanying fashions became feature stories in the nation's leading lifestyle magazines. Reed & Barton sterling was news.

Window display competitions for new sterling patterns among dealers offered grand trips and prizes for the winners and publicity for their business. During the 1960s promotional efforts included advertising in upscale magazines, sponsoring college scholarship contests, and promoting the company image as a fashion leader through movies made about silver, such as *How to Be a Successful Hostess,* and the sponsorship of a series of lectures about art and design. At high school home economics classes and on college campuses, young women registered for the sterling pattern of their choice, eager to be recipients of the prizes of sterling flatware, as starter sets, dessert servers, and the lapel pins that were distributed.

Women's colleges were solicited for the opinions of their students. The women were offered the incentive of winning a number of pieces in the pattern they picked, with the grand prize, a complete set of sterling. Gifts were distributed on every campus visited. A college silver opinion contest, in which each entry selected the Reed & Barton sterling she would like to receive as a prize, elicited thousands of applicants. As company representatives met and studied the preferences of prospective buyers, Reed & Barton was able to display its products on hundreds of college campuses. The young women educated about silver and expressing their pattern preference would soon be part of thousands of new households established throughout the country.

In 1949 Reed & Barton introduced the pattern *Burgundy* and successfully tied it into high fashion appeal. Couturier Henri Bendel designed a *Burgundy* evening gown and the company sent miniatures of the dress on manikins around the country to its dealers for window displays. *Burgundy* was a modification of the successful *Francis I* pattern without the fruit groupings and was affectionately named "fruitless Francis" by company staff. The new medium of television featured promotional advertising spots for the *Burgundy* pattern, a design that continues in current popularity. *Burgundy* brightly heralded the sterling success of the decade to come.

Evoking the Renaissance, Reed & Barton featured the skills of the silver crafts-

Florentine Lace design influenced women's fashions. 1951. Reed & Barton archives.

A variety of magazines read by women featured advertising for the sterling pattern *Silver Wheat* introduced in 1952. Reed & Barton archives.

man with the introduction in November 1951 of *Florentine Lace,* a distinctive pierced sterling pattern. *Florentine Lace* was heavily promoted and featured in newspapers nationwide by women's page editors, on radio and TV programs, and it became the subject of a newsreel release by Paramount News. *Florentine Lace* sterling became *Florentine Lace* fashion. The pattern reached a wide audience through displays in *Bride's Magazine, Charm, Gourmet, Harper's Bazaar, Ladies Home Journal, Mademoiselle, Town & Country Living,* and *Vogue,* promoting women's love for silver and lace. The modern craftsmanship of Reed & Barton had made this possible, and a six-piece place setting, including tax, sold for $38.50.

The State Institute of Art in Florence, Italy, sent a personally inscribed scroll of good wishes to all Reed & Barton dealers. Several hundred magazine and newspaper editors, radio and television personalities, and representatives of the Italian government were aboard the Italian luxury liner *Conte Biancamano* in New York Harbor as Colonel Arthur Ashworth, president of Reed & Barton, accepted a handsomely engraved jewel box from Italo Paini, the Italian consul for the City of Florence. The inscription read, "Well wishing to Reed & Barton Silversmiths, for their wonderful initiative in creating *Florentine Lace,* the magnificent new pierced pattern in sterling silver which represents the finest tradition in Italian Renaissance Art, thus linking modern American craftsmanship with the ancient City of Florence." Reed & Barton presented to the Art Institute in February 1952 a scholarship for an Italian student to learn the art of silversmithing.

In February 1952 the Fashion Academy awarded a gold medal to Reed & Barton "for the beauty of design and the excellent fashion styling" reflected in the sterling silver pattern of *Florentine Lace.* The award was based on the pattern's "artistic craftsmanship, inspirational authenticity and ingenious fashion appeal." The world's largest lace manufacturer, AMETEX (American Textile Company) was sufficiently inspired to design and name a lace pattern after it, transferring the acanthus leaf, rose, and scroll to gowns, blouses, gloves, and tablecloths. The world's designers were called upon to create new fashions; Jacques Fath, the Parisian couturier; Jane Derby, the winner of the 1951 Fashion Critics Award; and Marie of Pandora responded.

The following year *Silver Wheat* was introduced as part of the new "Ameri-

Advertisement for women's blouses, inspired by Reed & Barton's *Silver Wheat* sterling pattern, illustrates the coordinated lifestyle advertising campaign. Photographed from the *Silver Wheat* edition of *The Silver Lining,* November 1952. Reed & Barton archives.

cana" look in sterling. Wheat was "simple, fresh, and graceful," a part of American design as it was a symbol of America itself. *Silver Wheat* coordinated well with the new introduction of contemporary design in American home furnishings; *Silver Wheat* was at home in America. *Silver Wheat*'s inspiration was displayed in jewelry by Danecraft, dresses by Lotte of Drewyn, blouses by Gregory, separates by Nelly de Grab, and gowns by Fontana of Tafel. Window display contests were encouraged with bonus prize trips offered.

Reed & Barton's advertising campaign combined the ingredients of contemporary design, market research, high quality advertising, and promotion. A fashion show was held at the Hotel Pierre in New York City on 15 October 1952 featuring *Silver Wheat* inspired designs, which ranged from furs to sportswear. The company reported it to be "a glamorous affair." Editor of *American Home* magazine Gertrude Brassard had set a series of tables with *Silver Wheat* sterling to complement the different apparel styles. The pattern was successful in capturing the interest in contemporary fashion and represented the first success of a Reed & Barton pattern grouping known as *Romantic Modern,* which subsequently included *Classic Rose, Silver Sculpture,* and *Autumn Leaves.*

Classic Rose, introduced in 1954 with a college essay contest and actively promoted, accounted for almost a quarter of the company's total flatware sales that year and was to be the most enduring of the *Romantic Modern* patterns. In October 1954 *Silver Sculpture* was presented, in which the pattern design was sculptured from the metal itself, capturing the play of light and gleam of the sterling silver and incorporating the Scandinavian influence that was popular with Danish furniture of the period.

The pattern *Tara* arrived in the fall of 1955 and continues to be a popular sterling design. It reached first place in sales in 1956 and increased the company's distribution in the South, where Gorham traditionally had been strong. A week's cruise to Nassau for two aboard a luxury ship was the coveted grand prize in the *Tara* window display won by the S. L. Orr Co. of Macon, Georgia, in March 1956.

Achievement in innovative pattern design sparked Reed & Barton to invite a hands-across-the-ocean challenge by hiring well-known Italian architect Gio Ponti to design a flatware pattern. In addition to buildings, Ponti's designs encompassed modern furniture, automobiles, textiles, glassware, and ceramics. The result was the *Diamond* pattern that meshed Italian inspiration with Ameri-

Media advertisements of sterling patterns during the decade of the 1950s reflected a growing market for sterling sales. Circa 1956. Reed & Barton archives.

Inspired by nature are the patterns *Fleur-de-lis, Autumn Leaves, Classic Rose,* and *Silver Wheat.*

Above, The *Silver Sculpture* sterling flatware pattern was a breakthrough contemporary design when it was introduced in 1954.

Right, The delicate design of *Tara* made this sterling pattern an early and enduring success.

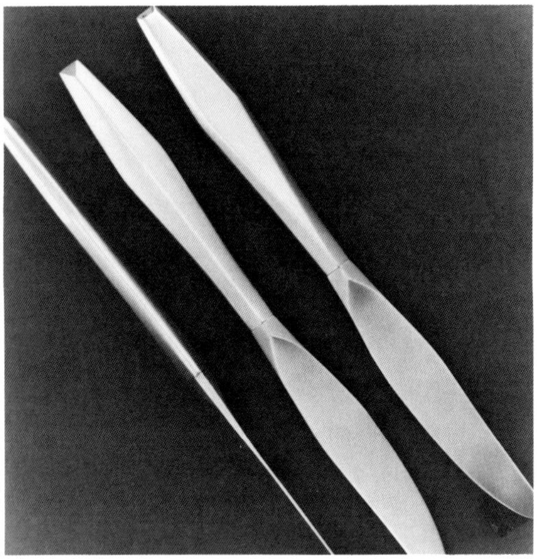

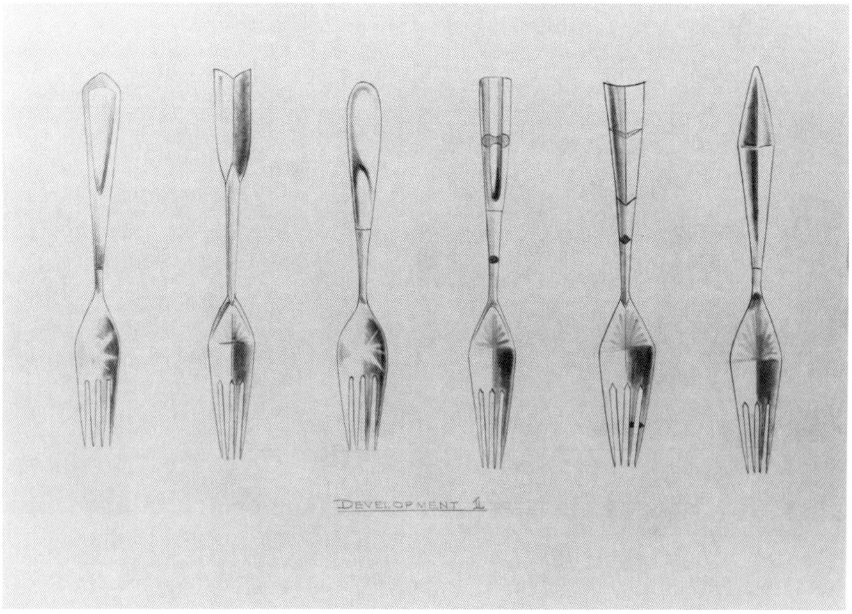

Ponti's asymmetric *Diamond* pattern was introduced in 1958 and required the challenge of new tools and manufacturing techniques to produce. Reed & Barton archives.

can ingenuity, as Ponti's design was adapted for the United States market by head designer Theodore Cayer. The innovative asymmetric *Diamond* pattern made its debut in 1958 as "the most advanced sterling of our generation" and was celebrated with a reception at the Plaza Hotel in New York on 13 January 1958.

Reed & Barton's interest in creating innovative designs led to the invitation of well-known Italian architect Gio Ponti to design a flatware pattern for the company. Reed & Barton archives.

But could the pattern be produced? To make this possible new tools and manufacturing techniques were required. The wedge-shaped handles of the forks and spoons could not be produced the way conventional flat-handled pieces are and a new stainless steel knife blade had to be created. In cross section the blade perfectly fits the diamond shape of the sterling handle. S. & G. Gump Company of San Francisco were the winners of the *Diamond* pattern window display contest, receiving a ten-day round trip to Italy with a first stop visit to the studio of the pattern's designer Gio Ponti in Milan.

The 1950s had been a decade of sterling that now defined the company. Shreve, Crump & Low in Boston honored the company's success with a *Salute to Reed & Barton* week at the beginning of April 1959. The 1950s were generally characterized at Reed & Barton by strong profits and steady sales and are remembered as a good time in the life of the company. Continued management succession in the Weeks family was assured when Sinclair "Sinny" Weeks Jr. joined the Board of Directors in 1959. The Quarter Century Club had 186 members in 1955, 136 of whom were active, resulting in a well-attended August clambake. The Bowling League attracted many members during the 1940s and 1950s, while the softball team performed well in the Industrial League. As one of the largest employers in town, Reed & Barton had the advantage of choosing from many of its townspeople.

The funding of a motion picture, *The Romance of Silver Design,* produced by Kenneth and Shirley Richter, and filmed in different countries, enabled Reed & Barton to reach a wider audience. The movie, originally intended for high school and college classes, women's clubs and similar organizations, was shown on television stations and reached an audience in the millions. It was also an effective sales presentation used by dealers and to teach sales personnel more about silver design.

Television conveyed the promotional excitement of contest winners receiving Reed & Barton silver before a large audience. The program *Bride and Groom,* with an audience estimated at twenty million per week, featured the marriage of a couple who received a Reed & Barton sterling silver service in the pattern of

A scene recreating the workshop of noted sixteenth-century silversmith Benvenuto Cellini, 1500–1571, in Florence, Italy, as a nobleman and his wife discuss commissioning his work. A still from the Reed & Barton movie, *The Romance of Silver Design,* directed by Richter Productions. 1953. Reed & Barton archives.

their choice, presented to them by the nearest dealer when they returned from their honeymoon.

A study by the Sterling Silversmiths Guild recommended group advertising as the market for sterling broadened. "In the days of the class market, the major factor of competition was from within, i.e., Wallace vs. International vs. Lunt vs. Reed & Barton and others. The carriage trade patron had a cultivated taste and demand for Sterling. To her, it was a question of *whose* Sterling. With the mass market it is no longer a foregone conclusion that the consumer wants Sterling Silverware. She must be encouraged to buy Sterling, its value and desirability impressed upon her. Will she buy Sterling or a fur coat?"

It was Reed & Barton's commitment to the Guild, and not problems with sterling sales, that led President Roger Hallowell to initiate a cooperative promotion to increase sales for all members. The effort proved a difficult one, but in 1957 Guild members supported a $400,000 national program of radio ads which inspired Denham Lunt Sr. to write to Sinclair Weeks Sr., then secretary of commerce in Washington, praising Hallowell's leadership in an industry that resisted unified direction. "Over the years, I know how many times you tried and I tried to get the industry to band together in doing constructive work. We accomplished something, but I know of no project that is as big, or, I feel, as promising as this program that Roger has successfully put through."

But the pressure to increase sales led one company after another to ignore the standard practices they had adopted, and discounting and cooperative advertis-

Senator John F. Kennedy and wife Jacqueline receive a sterling Paul Revere punch set made by Reed & Barton and purchased at the LaFrance Jewelry Company of New Bedford on behalf of the citizens of New Bedford and Fall River. The presentation was made by Edward Simmons of the *New Bedford Standard Times* at the twin-city testimonial. 1956. Reed & Barton archives.

ing became the future direction. By 1960 discount price promotion was the rule throughout the industry and Reed & Barton, the exception. Weeks continued to caution. "It's all right to compete on merchandise, but when you start competition on terms there is only one end to that road."

As president, Hallowell followed Sinclair Weeks in his opposition to price-cutting. "Reed & Barton has not taken part in any of this type of cut-price operations. It is our feeling that this type of promotion stimulates sales temporarily but, in the long run, confuses the customers and the trade as to what the real value of sterling flatware is and, in turn, tends to make the sale of our product very uneven throughout the year." But the direction of the industry was towards price-cutting. In 1964 the Sterling Silversmiths Guild commissioned a study to determine the effect price reductions would have on persuading consumers to increase their purchases or affect their opinion of silver as a valuable commodity. The study showed that few consumers had any idea of the price of silver or what particular items, such as a four-piece place setting, would cost, though most responded that they would buy more silver if the price were lower.

While other firms moved towards stainless steel and diverse product offerings, Reed & Barton continued its emphasis on sterling and its position as a leader in design. In February 1960 the sterling patterns *The Lark* and *Star*, created by designer John Prip, were introduced after considerable market research conducted through the Chicago Research Institute. Light and sleek in appearance, each pattern was described as having a distinctive personality appeal for women. *The Lark* was promoted for the "sophisticated modern" girl while *Star* was "romantic contemporary."

Roger Hallowell as President initiated an association with museums and design institutes to promote silver designers and educate the public. Circa 1955. Reed & Barton archives.

Prip developed a new finish called "Color Glaze" that proved to be a major innovation for the industry. Of Danish background, Prip was familiar with the popularity of enameled silver bowls in Scandinavian countries and proposed their introduction to Reed & Barton. The new Color Glaze finish featured gem-like colors and found a receptive market in January 1961. When sales reached $40,000 in a three-week period, the company knew that production, not sales, would be the greater concern. Though many firms attempted to copy the look, the Reed & Barton Color Glaze finish was distinctive.

Roger Hallowell as president initiated Reed & Barton's association with museums and design institutes to promote silver designers and educate the public about silver making. A series of lectures by internationally known designers, art

The brilliance of Color Glaze finish on Paul Revere bowls. 1961. Reed & Barton archives.

historians, and critics was held during the 1960s and included Sir Kenneth Clark at Wellesley College, Marcel Brauer at the University of Michigan, and Count Bernadotti at Sarah Lawrence. In 1979 a federally funded exhibition, titled "Silver in American Life," featured Reed & Barton pieces as it toured a dozen museums over a three-year period, portraying the cultural significance of silver over the centuries.

Many of the younger silver buyers preferred to shop at the department store rather than the jewelers. With the arrival of the suburban shopping mall during the 1960s and the proliferation of outlets, department stores came into their own. Market research showed that consumers bought 90 percent of all holloware as gifts and purchasers were looking for appearance rather than long-term use and wear. Catalogues and showrooms that promoted lower priced giftware adversely impacted high quality silver products of companies like Reed & Barton.

The 1960s began with promise but evolved as a time of social unrest and lifestyle change. The conventional norms and established lifestyle choices were no longer assured. After years of prominence, sterling was no longer guaranteed a place at the table.

C840590
999+ FINE SILVER 100 TR OZ

HAYWIRE: A TIME OF SPECULATIVE EXCESS

In an inflationary economy the highly liquid, hard asset investments of silver and gold have a special allure. Beginning in 1973, Bunker and Herbert Hunt of Texas began to invest their family's oil fortune heavily in silver bullion and futures. The objective of the Hunt brothers, along with their Saudi Arabian associates, was to control the price of world silver by cornering the market.

In 1979 they came uncomfortably close to succeeding. By the time silver had reached an incomprehensible $50 an ounce in January 1980, it had become a commodity to be traded. In the aftermath, irreplaceable legacies of sentiment and skill, craftsmanship and culture, were lost forever in the stampede to the smelter.

The silver buying speculation endangered the world's large brokerage houses and the major banks within the United States and Switzerland that had extended their credit. When the price began to fall, brokers required cash to cover the reduced value of the futures contracts; and as the frenetic need to cover margin continued, no one could predict the outcome. The public's faith in the worth of silver was shattered.

Silver with all the trimmings. A display of fine metal ingots, collectible ingots, coins, and trimmings. Courtesy of the Gold & Silver Institutes, Washington, D.C.

Industry leaders helplessly posted successive price increases, and as Sinclair Weeks Jr., president of Reed & Barton during this time, relates, "The damage inflicted has never fully healed. It was a time of tremendous danger and strain. The mystique, formerly associated with silver, gave way to confusion surrounding its honest price and value." With the cost of silver remaining relatively high and unstable and without reasonable protective tariff and quota arrangements

Newspaper headlines relate the impact of speculative buying in silver. Reed & Barton archives.

High prices tarnish sterling silver sales

NEW YORK — If you see an ad saying "Big silverware sale, 70 percent off list price!," take it with a grain of salt. The silver business is infected with list prices well above the usual selling price, according to several retailers. One store's heavily advertised sale price may be the same as another store's regular price.

A New York store recently advertised a silverware sale that included Towle's Old Master pattern. The list price was $530 for a four-piece setting. The store's sale price was $159, which appears to be 70 percent off. But a Towle spokesman says the Old Master setting commonly sells for around $265, so the true discount was more like 40 percent. That's still a good deal, but not as good as the ad made it sound.

Retailer Joanne Levi, of Cruckemeyer & Cohn in Evansville, Ind., says silverware often sells for about half the suggested list price. In these cases, the discount would have to be more than 50 percent before you're getting a true bargain. All in all, it's a bad situation for the consumer. Unless you take the time to shop around, you can't tell what the true level of silverware prices is today.

silver plate have not been very imaginative or varied. But with more young couples giving up on the idea of sterling, manufacturers should respond with more and better designs.

There's no fixed amount of silver in silver plate. Manufacturers make their own determination. A common choice might be 7½ percent silver, electrically bonded to a base metal like brass, nickel or copper. Sterling, by contrast, is 92½ percent silver and 7½ percent copper or other metals. A five-piec[e] place setting of silver plate might run in t[he] area of $50.

● Sterling II, a product of Wallace S[ilver]smith. The handles are sterling; the blade, fork and spoon end are stainle[ss]. A place setting might cost $120, with $245 for a comparable setti[ng in ster]ling silver.

● Gold-plated flatware. Acc[ording to] New York Bridal Registry, Ltd., sales of gold-plated f[latware ...] sharply since September, a[s couples] explore alternatives to [...] place setting of 24-carat [...] less steel is selling for $[...]

● Pewter. Kirk-St[ieff ...] turer of pewterwar[e ...]

Sterling Out of Reach For Many Brides

By EMILIE TAVEL LIVEZEY
Christian Science Monitor

TAUNTON, Mass. — Sterling silver hasn't priced itself entirely out of the market yet, but it's trying.

There are people—plenty of them—who still can afford this "queen of metals," treasured down through the ages for its reflective beauty.

But your run-of-the-mill wedding guest, choosing a gift for a June bride, soon will find out, if he hasn't been in a jewelry store recently, that he's out of the sterling silver ballpark. He probably will end up with silver plate, known technically as hollowares.

A set of genuine sterling today costs as much as a house did a generation or so ago. Sterling tea services, for example, begin at about $3,000 and run up to a dizzying $19,000.

In the same patterns, excellent quality plated tea services range from $800 to $1,200.

A sterling place setting long has been a traditional bridal gift. But with six pieces of sterling now going for $300 to $600, plated flatware at $80 to $90 a setting is more within reach.

A lot of wedding guests probably turn to what the vast majority of Americans now are eating with — stainless steel flatware.

The bride who does receive sterling today will instinctively get the message: Somebody who could afford to really went overboard for her.

Until 1962 the price of silver was less than $1 an ounce. Then it took off, leap-

Market conditions have driven many manufacturers almost entirely out of the sterling business. Some have only a few small pieces left in their catalogs — such as baby cups priced from $200 to $300, marketed mainly to doting grandparents.

Even Reed & Barton here in Taunton, the old and distinguished company that introduced electroplating to the United States from England in the 1850s, is not offering as wide a variety of sterling holloware items as it once did.

Yet George M. Gregory, director of marketing services, says it never ceases to amaze him how many of its hand-chased Francis I sterling tea services sell at $19,150.

"We still look at it as a very good business," he says, adding that even though the company's unit volume of sterling flatware has gone down, the dollar volume has gone up and still is its largest business.

Twenty years ago silver sales at Boston's Shreve, Crump & Low Co., the Tiffany and Cartier of New England, were running 80 percent sterling and 20 percent plate. Today it's 40 percent sterling and 60 percent plate.

Shreve's caters to collectors, designs its own sterling objets d'art, deals in costly museum-piece reproductions and says it offers the largest selection of sterling tea services in the nation.

But it realizes that sterling is beyond the reach of many, so Donald C. Thomas, manager of the silver department, is scouring the world market for the best in plated ware.

against foreign imports of stainless steel, the domestic silver market was further weakened.

The rise in silver prices from 1973 through 1975 was accompanied by increases in other basics in the economy, such as in gasoline and food; and consumers adjusted to the new level. The market began to rise dramatically during 1978 as speculative pressure by the Hunt brothers increased. Bill Dykstra became treasurer at Reed & Barton in April 1978 when silver was increasing in price and the sterling business was shrinking. The company, he recalls, reacted to the wide price swings by purchasing millions of ounces of silver during the low points, aware that even a ten-cent rise significantly impacted profits. In 1979 silver prices showed a low of $5.93 and a high of $35.00.

Bill Dykstra was Chief Financial Officer of Reed & Barton during the period of speculation and rising silver prices. 1980. Reed & Barton archives.

Privately owned silver was being sold because of its sudden increase in value. Reed & Barton purchased some of this silver from "brokers" who were buying it from individual owners. The company paid about 40 percent of the silver's value when it arrived and sent it directly to the refineries for credit or cash. Reed & Barton received a ready supply of silver, relates Dykstra, recalling "the armored trucks arriving at the factory to deliver as many as 10,000 ounces of sterling to be converted to 9,000 ounces of fine silver. We had easy access to selling silver. I would sell the silver pieces the same day during the six to eight weeks of this bubble. Handy & Harman was the metal fabricator for our specs and we told them what form we wanted the silver to be. We always returned silver scrap to them for immediate credit. Occasionally we got stuck with silver pieces that wouldn't sell."

While Dykstra ably faced the challenge of this "chaotic, wild time," he laments "the loss of beautiful handiwork by artisans no longer around." People were afraid to use sterling, and criminal break-ins were rising. Bill Hurley had his Taunton home broken into several times.

Prices rose frequently, "sometimes twice a week on flatware," relates Dykstra. New price lists were needed to reflect the increasing cost of silver, "a monumental task and one in which it was very easy for mistakes to occur," remembers Richard Gillespie, vice president of sales at the time. In their news about the silver industry on 9 January 1980, United Press International wire service relayed Gillespie's remarks that Reed & Barton's 1 January prices became obsolete on 2 January.

Craig Francis, who thought he had seen it all in his lengthy sales career with Reed & Barton, can only describe 1979–80 as an "off the wall" time. "In the beginning when price increases were gradual, consumers continued buying, motivated by the investment aspect. It was the only time in my experience that volume went up when prices went up. But in 1979 the spreadsheet showed we had nine price increases. To see beautiful sterling waiters, some engraved with priceless sentiment, such as the one I saw from the people of the city of LeHavre, France, in appreciation for being liberated during World War II, selling for scrap was heartbreaking. People were irrational with their possessions."

When the commodity exchange put an end to further trading in silver futures, the silver bubble for speculators burst, and the market fell in March 1980 to eleven dollars an ounce. Reed & Barton lowered its prices as the cost of silver fell, but others in the industry delayed doing so and instead advertised large dis-

Sterling Flatware List Prices, 1978–1997

4-Piece Place Setting (*Francis I* and *18th-Century*)

	suggested retail price
October 1978	$230.00
December 1978	$230.00
January 1979	$230.00
February 1979	$230.00
March 1, 1979	$257.00
April 30, 1979	$257.00
May 29, 1979	$294.00
September 5, 1979	$385.00
September 19, 1979	$560.00
November 19, 1979	$560.00
January 7, 1980	$730.00
February 1, 1980	*$998.00
July 21, 1980	$630.00
November 17, 1980	$780.00
March 22, 1981	$356.00
May 17, 1981	$228.00
August 2, 1981	$332.00
November 1, 1981	$332.00
August 1, 1982	$260.00
January 24, 1983	$336.00
March 1, 1990	$330.00
January 1, 1995	$345.00
January 1, 1997	$345.00

*Spreadsheet with nine price groups from $998 to $1436 was distributed to dealers. The price the dealer paid was dependent on the cost of silver bullion. Reed & Barton would advise customers which price group to refer to.

counts and promotional gifts. Since the suggested retail prices were not being used, Reed & Barton considered the practice deceptive. "Amidst the free snow blowers, TVs, and other giveaways was very fictitious pricing," relates Gillespie.

Reed & Barton had traditionally opposed marketing silver through discounting, and Bill Hurley promoted the importance of design instead. "It's really the pattern that counts." Weeks observes that retail prices had become meaningless. "It was time to reestablish realistic pricing for this time-honored product and to reassert the basic values of sterling flatware through sound advertising and merchandising programs which are based on the product's innate elegance and appeal to the American consumer." The industry's jewelry store customers had been particularly hurt by the heavy promotional discount activity.

Reed & Barton found itself alone, as its competitors in the Sterling Silversmiths Guild refused to reduce their suggested retail prices when the price of silver came down and increased their discounts instead. "The angst of discounting" was indeed hurting the company's business, relates Senior Vice President of Marketing and Business Development Tony LaChapelle. During the 1981 fall New York trade show, Reed & Barton took action with the publication of a full-page ad in the November eighth issue of the *New York Times* showing two virtually identical forks, one from Reed & Barton, the other from a competitor.

The advertisement graphically illustrated the pricing disparity and confusion. The suggested retail price of a competitor's fork at $215.00, even with a 60 percent discount, was $86.00, while the Reed & Barton fork, with a list price of $90.00, sold for $67.50 after a 25 percent discount.

Business Week observed in its 29 March 1982 issue that "deep discounting–selling merchandise to customers at 40–85 percent below the manufacturer's 'suggested retail price' has embroiled the United States silver industry in a bitter controversy that has tarnished the silversmith's reputation and left customers confused about the actual value of silverware. One of the most prestigious names in silverware, Reed & Barton Corporation, is taking on most of the industry in a legal battle, charging five competitors with false advertising concerning the price of their products."

There was no winner, no gain for anyone. "The market has never fully recovered," reflects Craig Francis. "Sterling lost its shine, its allure. There was no longer an image of stability; a lot of the romance of sterling was lost." At Reed & Barton, the company's dependency on the sterling business in a market of shrink-

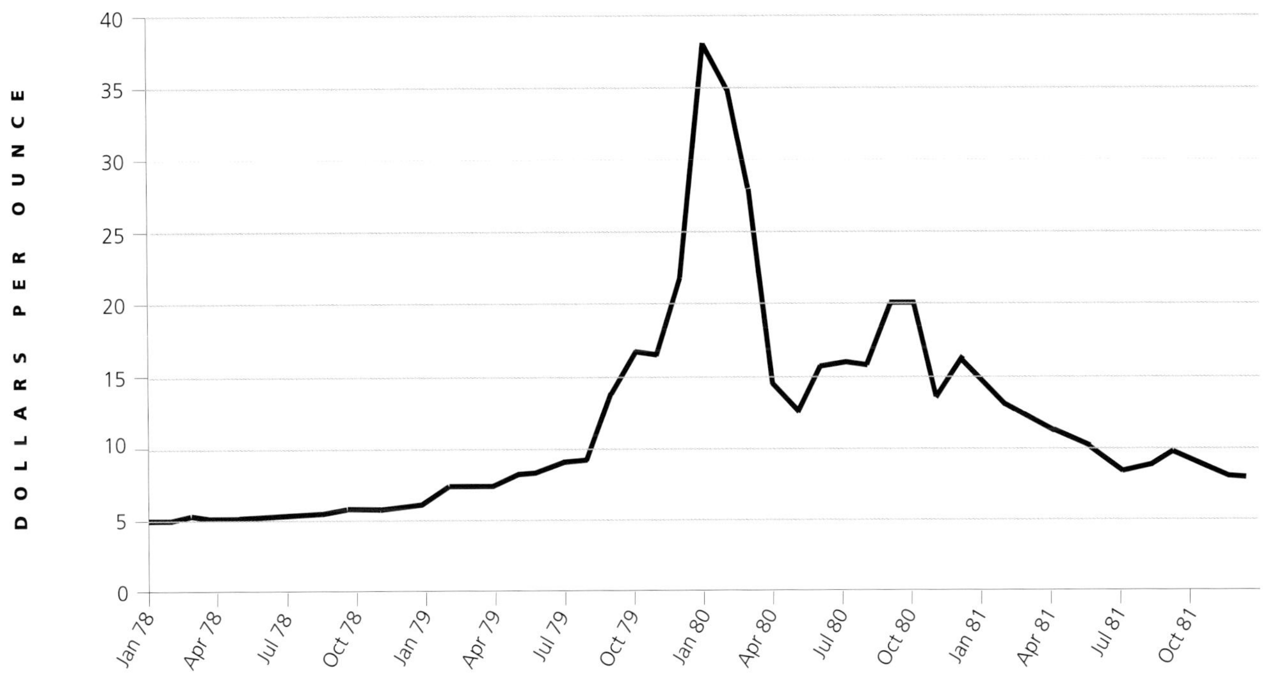

Handy and Harman Monthly Average Silver Price per Troy Ounce

Data courtesy of Mr. Walter Frankland, Silver Users Association, Washington, D.C.

ing volume had left it vulnerable and led to the long-term decision to develop new product and distribution lines. One source of business was the result of the lawless aftermath of spiked silver prices. For well into the 1980s, Reed & Barton silversmiths were busy manufacturing replacements for claims processed by insurance companies for silver that had been stolen.

MARKETING AND SALES were the wheels of the company for Senior Vice President of Marketing and Business Development Tony LaChapelle when he first arrived in 1970 just out of college. "Tap Osborn was the Director of Advertising then, responsible for the company's image making. He was brilliant, mercurial, and one of the best writers I have met. In the early 1970s I spent days writing a handful of product descriptions until I satisfied him. He recognized the power of advertising and the need to be in touch with the consumer."

The heyday of Reed & Barton introducing new patterns as a grand media opening night event was passing to a new era of casual indifference to past traditions and even determined defiance by some of the nation's youth. But before it was over, LaChapelle was able to experience the excitement for himself and appreciate stories told of the past two decades when sterling drove the company. "I remember going with Tap for the presentation of a new pattern to the Four Seasons restaurant in New York City with at least 150 people present. The press kits were distributed, and the excitement built until the big moment when the pattern was finally unveiled."

There was the glamour of endorsements from Hollywood stars and celebrities, smiling as brilliantly as the Reed & Barton silver, commemorating the special occasion. "The 1950s, 1960s, and early 1970s were the years of the big promotional parties and salesmen carrying expensive velvet lined cases," relates LaChapelle. "A sterling pattern was an integral part of the American lifestyle, as much a part of the wedding as the gown. The sterling pattern that we introduced each year created excitement among our staff and the retailers who carried the line."

Eighty-four pieces of *Francis I* flatware displaying the fifteen varying fruit designs. Reed & Barton archives.

Reed & Barton launched its broadest national advertising campaign in 1960

Stafford "Tap" Osborn, *left*, and Tony LaChapelle discuss marketing strategy. 1974. Reed & Barton archives.

Right, Martini shaker appeared in *The New Yorker* magazine ad campaign. January 1971. Reed & Barton archives.

through leading magazines, most of which were directed to women, reaching an estimated 125 million. One hundred advertisements appeared in color and black-and-white in the magazines of *Vogue, Glamour, Mademoiselle, Seventeen, Living for Young Homemakers, House and Garden, House Beautiful, The New Yorker, Town and Country, Gourmet, Bride's,* and *Bride & Home.* The advertisements departed from the traditional representation in the silverware industry featuring a variety of designs to a single pattern campaign. Each ad would have its exclusive presentation and not appear opposite another ad. A single piece of holloware, beautifully photographed, graced the pages of *The New Yorker, Town & Country,* and *Gourmet.*

The New Yorker ad campaign was effectively created by the advertising agency of Ogilvy & Mather in New York City with Osborn and Hurley in charge of advertising and marketing, respectively. Reed & Barton's ad appeared within the first ten pages of each issue thirteen times a year, says LaChapelle. "The prominent placement of the ad gave the reader the appearance of viewing the company's product in every issue. The impression was one of quality and distinction and our image was enhanced by this campaign."

A highlight for LaChapelle was working with Osborn on the Classic American Silver campaign that defined the company's image. "The Classic American Silver" became on 12 May 1981 a registered trademark for Reed & Barton sterling and silverplated products. Regardless of the pattern being featured, the message was recognizable to the reader.

The advertising agency of Humphrey, Browning, and McDougall in Boston originated the campaign through its creative directors Mary Moore and Cheryl Heller. "They were smart young women, who loved silver and could see the potential of the product. 'Classic American Silver' is so simple and so descriptive. We introduced photographs of things that were American classics. One ad presented a patchwork quilt, Clark Gable and Vivian Leigh in a scene from *Gone with the Wind,* and a jeep as recognizable associations to the Reed & Barton place setting that was featured. It clicked well and received a lot of attention. My strategy in advertising is that the product has to be the hero and the brand name has to be prominent," says LaChapelle.

While it is usually difficult to measure the effectiveness of national advertising, observes LaChapelle, Moore and Heller successfully used the promotion for the sterling pattern *18th Century,* which was created by John Gilroy, the com-

The sterling flatware pattern *18th Century* became a best seller when it was advertised through the Classic American Silver campaign in 1983. Reed & Barton archives.

The sterling pattern *Pointed Antique* appeared in the Classic American Silver advertising campaign, which helped define the company's image. The Classic American Silver became a registered trademark for Reed & Barton silver in 1981. Reed & Barton archives.

Talented designer John Gilroy created a number of company products, including the popular *18th Century* sterling flatware pattern. 1974. Reed & Barton archives.

pany's head designer, and introduced in 1971. "It was a fairly contemporary pattern, but had started quite slowly. When we started advertising it in the Classic American Silver campaign in 1983, the pattern took off dramatically and soon became the number one selling sterling pattern in the United States. It was, and still remains, one of the best selling sterling patterns in the country, second in our total sales to *Francis I.* No other company had produced a fluted pattern; it was almost contemporary in appearance and spawned a lot of knockoffs." In the late 1980s there were modifications in ad presentations, but the Classic American Silver identification for Reed & Barton products endured. Placement up front in the *New York Times Magazine,* considered "the centerpiece in advertising," says LaChapelle, was something to be fought for and for which he worked hard to successfully negotiate.

Reed & Barton continues as an important source of high-end giftware. By the mid 1970s there was considerable pressure within the company to bring in new products and diversify. "The outreach was trendy, a fashion business, with products coming and going," says LaChapelle. In 1978, for example, John Gilroy and Dick Gillespie, vice president of marketing, introduced "the height of running chic," a silver-tipped jogging stick. The fourteen-inch-long varnished walnut

Damascene plate portraying New England village life, Christmas collection 1976, and Damascene jewelry, spring collection 1982, utilized a process of etching and the depositing of layers of copper, brass, and silver to create a three-dimensional effect of changing color and tone. Reed & Barton archives.

stick sold for twenty dollars and was described "as the ultimate measure of defense against canine and car, and called the 'Run for Your Life Jogging Stick.'"

In 1970 an ancient art form became a new medium in silverplated holloware for Reed & Barton. Robert Johnson, a textile designer, introduced the Damascene collection, first as collectors' plates and then as jewelry. Modern techniques were applied to the ancient craft that flourished in Damascus. Johnson had developed a process of etching and depositing layers of copper, brass, and silver that combined to create a three-dimensional effect of continuously changing color and tone. Adding a black nickel oxide, which could be contained in the crevices but polished off exposed surfaces, the designs could be outlined, just as complex patterns on silver holloware were delineated.

President Roger Hallowell had seen Johnson's Damascene works exhibited, and he was hired to work with Bill Hurley and Tap Osborn to develop products using the Damascene process. Early in 1970 Johnson began to transfer his equipment to Taunton. The introduction of the 1970 "Limited Edition" Christmas plate was an immediate success with demand exceeding the available supply. The Limited Edition plates were serially numbered and included reproductions of Audubon birds. Hurley extended the market to direct mail merchandisers such as American Heritage and the Danbury Mint. Marshall Field & Co. of Chicago

Equestrian Braid, 18/8 stainless steel, inspired by leather saddle braids and the tradition of the hunt. Flatware is manufactured under licensed agreement with Ralph Lauren's Home Collection. 1992. Reed & Barton archives.

commissioned limited editions of special or regional market pieces, such as the Chicago Water Tower, as did Shreve, Crump & Low in Boston. The Danbury Mint ordered 7,500 sterling silver "Winter" plates, and the Montana Historical Society ordered 2,500 plates illustrating a Charles Russell western scene.

The process was expanded to wall plaques, and when the interest in collectors' plates and art plaques ebbed, moderately priced Damascene jewelry was successfully marketed during the late 1970s and early 1980s. "At the height of its business, we were doing four to five million dollars in Damascene products," relates LaChapelle. "The popularity of the product eventually diminished because it was so fashion oriented."

In the early 1980s to stay competitive the company broadened both its product line and price points. "Our stated objective was to make and sell products that today's market will buy," says LaChapelle. "We increased our sales of stainless flatware and succeeded in securing 10 to 15 percent of the national market; we sold porcelain statues and Damascene jewelry. Our competitive advantage became product design." As vice president of merchandising, Osborn developed

Silver for children is a growing part of the giftware business. "Bunnykins" products were produced in 1998 by Reed & Barton under licensed agreement with Royal Doulton. Reed & Barton archives.

Above, Selection of Christmas ornaments from the 1997 collection. Reed & Barton archives.

Right, Selection of silver-plated giftware. 1995. Reed & Barton archives.

Popular Reed & Barton stainless patterns *Longwood, left,* and *Hammered Antique.* The growth of sales for stainless flatware reflects the market's informal lifestyle and the company's appealing pattern designs. Reed & Barton archives.

and expanded the line of engraveables and specialties, such as bookmarks and business card holders that sold in the ten to twenty-five dollar range; Damascene plates and limited edition pieces and Damascene jewelry; and Christmas ornaments, such as the Christmas Cross, which grew in demand to become a separate product category in the early 1980s.

During the 1970s the company recognized that manufacturing stainless flatware in Taunton was no longer price competitive. The first stainless flatware manufactured abroad was the *Diamante* pattern in Japan in 1979. The design for *Diamante* was based on the sterling pattern *Diamond,* first presented in 1958. In 1983 Reed & Barton introduced two of the company's top stainless patterns, *1800* and *Country French.*

Through increased outsourcing, Reed & Barton became a distributor and importer; that meant learning the culture and players abroad, explains LaChapelle. "We knew how to manufacture but had to turn to the Far East for lower labor costs. I had a lot of pride in what we did and it was very difficult to go abroad and provide our technical expertise especially if they were going to sell to our competitors. We were used to making products within the walls of Reed & Barton and it was a difficult culture shock. Reed & Barton workers had been for so long the die makers, toolmakers, solderers, spinners, chasers, and silversmiths. The company manufactures a lot less than we used to, and gradually since the late 1980s we have done more product development and distribution, and less manufacturing in Taunton."

Reed & Barton now offers a variety of price points for its stainless flatware patterns, categorized by the three primary lines of *Legacy, Cuisine,* and *Luxury.* For the first time, in 1996, revenue from the sale of stainless flatware moved ahead of sterling flatware, the company's traditional primary revenue producer. Reed & Barton is now one of the largest producers and distributors of stainless flatware. With a market share of 11 to 12 percent, the company is second to Oneida, which has dominated the stainless industry. "In stainless Reed & Barton is high end and provides the same quality it has been known for in sterling and silverplate," says LaChapelle.

"During the 1980s and 1990s the retail landscape was in turmoil with consolidations and leveraged buyouts," relates LaChapelle. "We pulled our advertising back. With marketing you can either push the product through by aggressive marketing to the retailer, or pull the product through by advertising in the me-

Design Director Clark Lofgren sculpting the 1996 Olympic medal for the Summer Centennial Games. Display of gold, silver, and bronze medals with pictogram of each athletic event on the back. Reed & Barton archives.

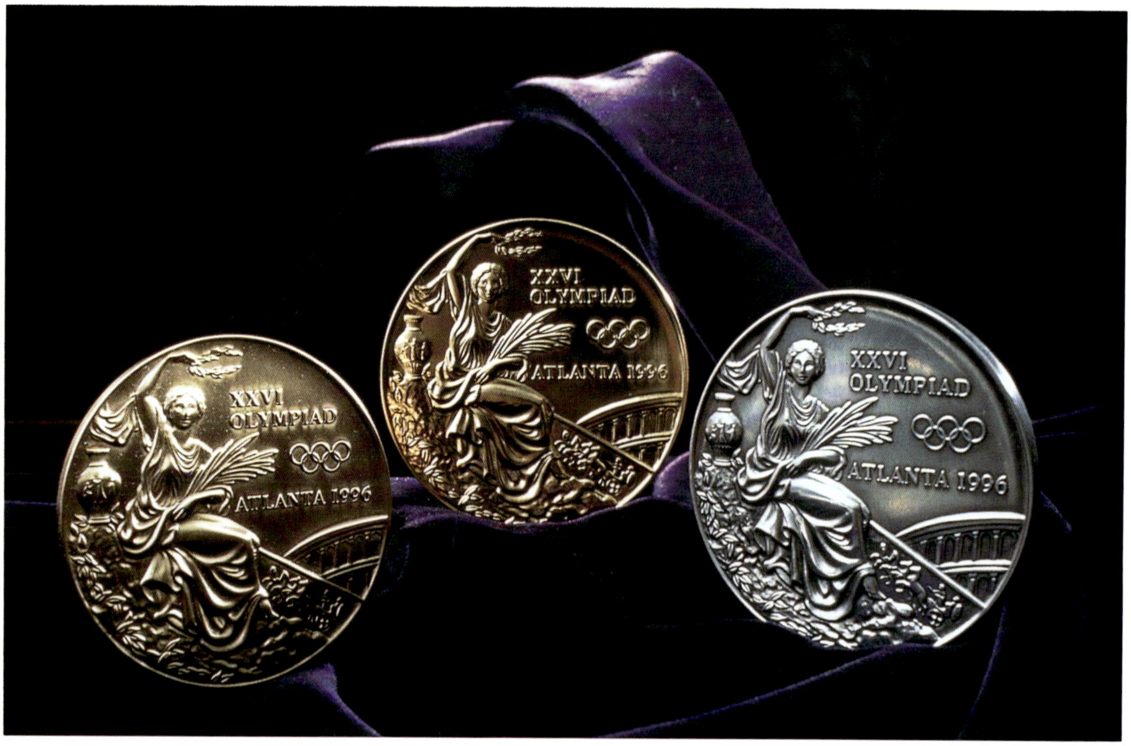

dia to reach the consumer, which we primarily did in the 1950s. Today the company does much less national advertising and the dollar focus has shifted to cooperative advertising with our retail customers whom we reimburse for their media ads. We are pushing our products through the retailer to the consumer. Our message to our retailers has been consistency; they know what we are about. There is a lot of continuity in the ranks of Reed & Barton's top management.

"Today's marketing approach is to find products that are directed to our target customer and fit well in our distribution channels. We try to find products to mix that take advantage of synergies of the two companies. A chest company like Eureka, a china company like Belleek, and a crystal company like Miller Rogaska offer high end, branded merchandise which appeals to the same retail customers who are reached through similar channels of distribution as Reed & Barton's traditional products."

Licensing agreements under which Reed & Barton sells flatware for Ralph Lauren and Waterford, and the children's "Bunnykins" line of Royal Doulton, add to the company's appeal and importance to the retailer, says LaChapelle. "It is all about establishing your sustainable competitive advantage."

The 1996 Olympic Games in Atlanta, Georgia, marked the centennial of the modern Olympic Games, drawing more than 10,000 athletes from over 200 countries. The stirring sounds of pageant, feats of performance, and triumph of victory for their winners have a cherished commemorative in the prestigious Olympic medals.

On 10 October 1995 the Atlanta Committee for the Olympic Games announced that Reed & Barton would receive the contract to supply the gold, silver, and bronze Olympic medals. The company was also licensed to produce Olympic Games giftware made of sterling, silverplate, goldplate, and wood. Reed & Barton had already established a working relationship with the Olympic Committee as an official Olympic licensee in December 1994. For the first time the medals had a keepsake case for display and storage, produced by Eureka Manufacturing, a division of Reed & Barton, which traditionally manufactures wooden silverware and jewelry boxes. In addition 52,600 bronze commemorative medals were manufactured by Reed & Barton for distribution by the Olympic committee.

The participation of Reed & Barton as the manufacturer of the Olympic medals was indeed a historic event for the company. At Reed & Barton months of excited and frenetic preparation preceded the games, as 1,926 medals were produced and readied for shipment. The Olympic Committee set strict production controls and time frames for delivery. Security was tight at the plant; the media flocked to Taunton, and LaChapelle and President Albert D. Krebel were ready for prime time interviews.

"Few projects have the honor and prestige of the Olympic medals," says LaChapelle. "It gives our people a chance to show their skills and the quality of their work to millions of people." Each medal produced was unique. For the first time pictograms representing the thirty-one athletic events were included on the back of the medals.

Krebel compared the historic tradition of the Olympics with that of Reed & Barton itself. "I find it especially significant that an American silver company with a 172-year history of business excellence produced the Olympic medals for this centennial event. This is a tremendous honor and fits into all the skills Reed & Barton has." The company faced strong competition to secure the contract among eight other manufacturers.

Measuring seven centimeters in diameter and five millimeters thick, the medals were polished with volcanic ash from Italy and buffed and rebuffed. The 637 gold medals were sterling silver clad with 22-karat gold fill covered by 24-karat gold plate; the 639 silver medals were made of solid sterling silver, and the 671 bronze medals of solid bronze. Extra medals were made in preparation for a tie in certain events.

The design elements on the front of the Victory medal are similar to the original introduced in 1928. Lady Victory is seated holding an olive wreath overhead with a bundle of palm leaves in her lap. There are images of ancient Greece that include an urn, the horse-drawn chariot, and the Olympic stadium. The addition of the Olympic Games rings on the front of the medal distinguish the centennial medals from those awarded in previous years.

Malcolm Grear of Providence, Rhode Island, was selected by the Olympic Committee to design the medals. Lady Victory appears more comely than in past renditions, with Clark Lofgren, design director at Reed & Barton, improving upon her facial features; and deeper sculpting adds more form to the figure. He describes it "as an inspiring project that had the whole company excited and was certainly a high point for me."

Medallion art was a familiar part of Lofgren's work. An accomplished sculptor, Lofgren modeled by hand each medal in clay. Three-dimensional plaster models, three times the actual size, were made of the medal's front and back. Each model was reduced to the exact size required to be cast in steel. A die was made from each steel casting, and the front and back of each medal was formed by stamping a blank metal disk between steel dies. Each medal blank was struck three times with over 600 tons of force to make the impression. Between each strike the medals were put through an annealing process with intense heat. Each medal was buffed, polished, and inspected at each step of the manufacturing process. Holes for ribbon holders were drilled approximately ¼ inch deep and the ribbons sewn at Eureka, a Reed & Barton subsidiary in Norton, Massachusetts. To guard against souvenir hunters or counterfeiters, all molds were broken after production.

The presence of Olympic Committee staff at Reed & Barton to assist in the distribution and shipping of the medals could only be likened to a military operation, relates LaChapelle. With 5,400 estimated man-hours of staff time involved in the production and packaging of the medals, Reed & Barton felt closely connected to the Summer Olympic Games. "It was great for our employees," said LaChapelle. "When they saw the winners, representing the best in their class, wearing the medals made at Reed & Barton, they could say, 'I was a part of that.'"

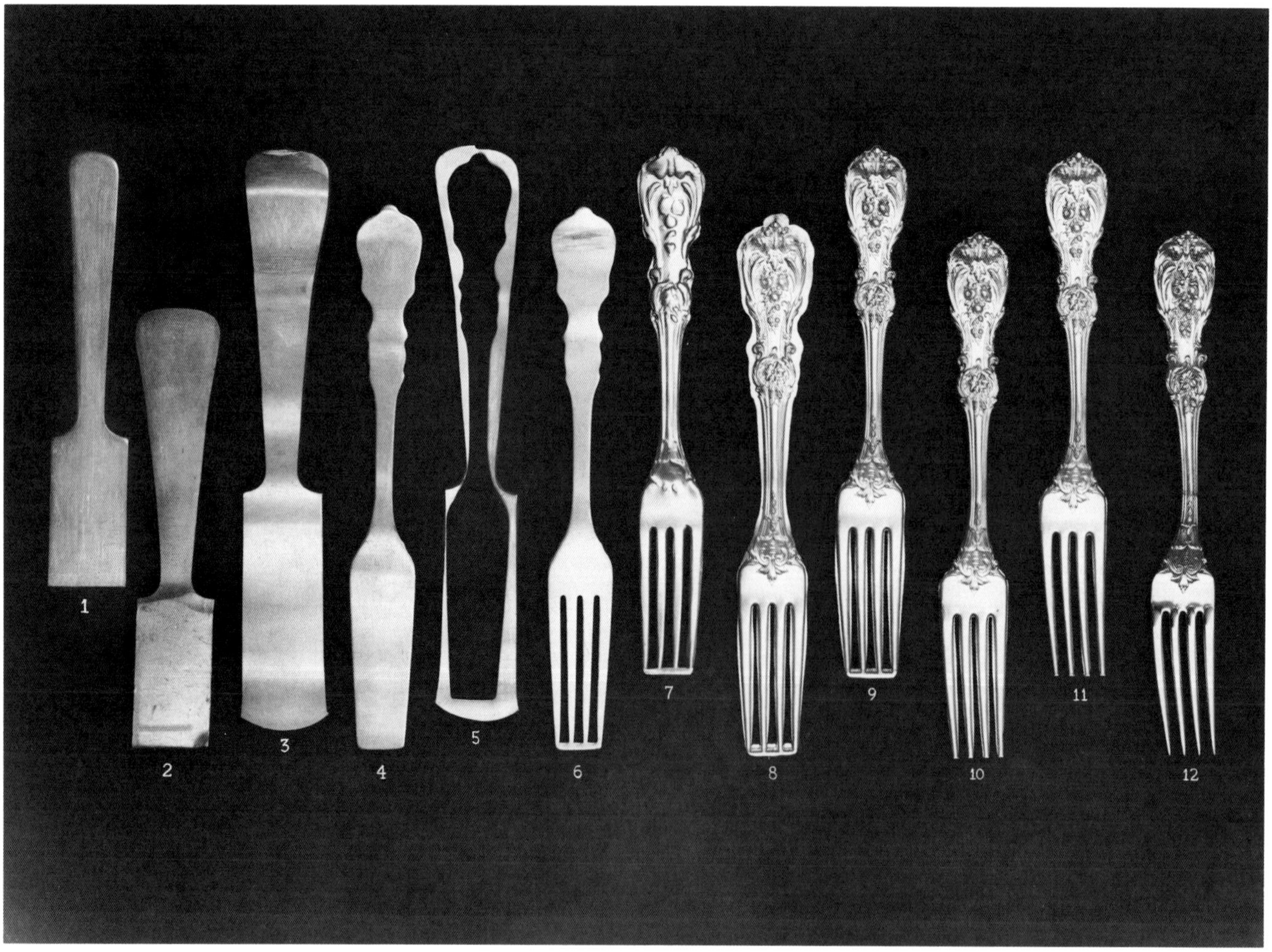
1
2
3
4
5
6
7
8
9
10
11
12

PLANT SUPERINTENDENT Herb "Butch" Leonard grew up in the Reed & Barton neighborhood and came to the company following graduation from high school in 1959. His father had worked in the foundry manufacturing castings, and other family members were employed by the company. "A lot of my relatives passed through these doors. This was the preferred place in town to work." Leonard knows manufacturing operations from the bottom up.

Many of the workers have relatives at Reed & Barton, explains Leonard. They are highly motivated, close-knit and local, from Taunton, Fall River, and New Bedford. He has experienced the changes from hand to automatic machinery, which have allowed the company to become more competitive but reduced the labor force required. "Up until the mid to late 1970s, flatware was finished by hand. On the factory floor sterling flatware is our mainstay; we offer a great variety of patterns. Christmas products and ornaments have become a big part of the business." Making the tools is still an essential part of manufacturing, he adds.

Though the company imports most of its stainless flatware, Leonard takes pride in the continued popularity of the *Colonial Shell* pattern that is made in Taunton. "It is difficult to be competitive in stainless manufacturing, but I don't like to see production going out and I'm glad when you can still make something here. Our backbone is still sterling flatware." He enjoys the company outreach with the Taunton community and the interest shown by school tours and local visiting groups in how the company's products are made.

Henry Gill's career at Reed & Barton from 1953 to 1990, starting as sales assistant and retiring as president of Reed & Barton Silversmiths, encompassed the heyday of expansion for the company and the silver industry, as well as

The operations of stamping a *Francis I* fork include from *left to right:* (1) the blank; (2) cross-rolled blank; (3) grade-rolled blank; (4) outlined blank; (5) scrap left after outlining blank; (6) tined blank; (7) form-stamped; (8) finish-stamped; (9) fork after removal of flash; (10) tine bar removed; (11) burrs removed from tines; (12) finished fork. In addition to stamping, other operations are employed to bring a fork to its finished state. Reed & Barton archives.

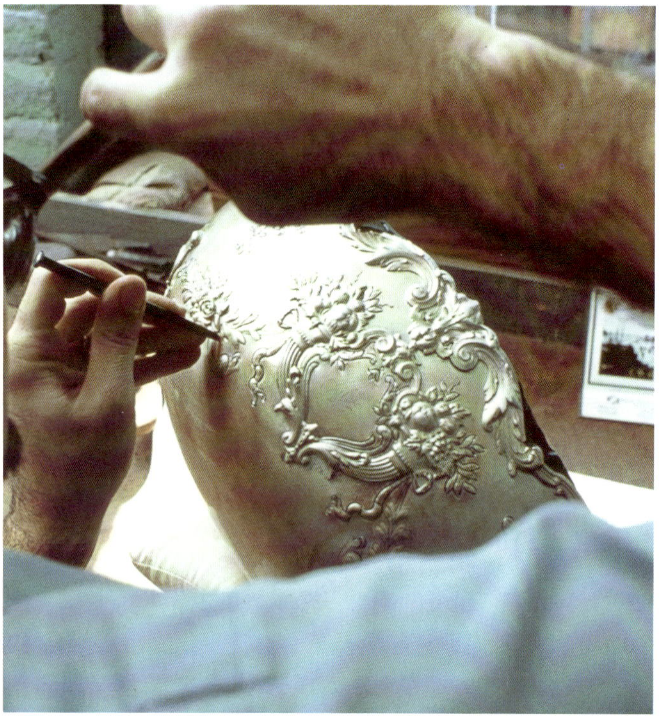

diversification through acquisition and licensing agreements. When Gill first arrived eager to apply his economics degree freshly minted from Harvard College, there were nine silver companies nationally and it was an exciting time of growth. "Reed & Barton was known for its premier quality and name and there was a gentlemanly style of doing business. It was an energetic, fun time. We worked and socialized together within the industry. We were growing with sterling as our main product line. Our market share increased by having good patterns and the key to our success was excellence in design, which kept us growing until the 1970s."

The sterling service order from the Saudi Arabian government in 1980 stands out in its size, scope, and daunting challenge. "Without question it has to be the largest single order we have ever filled," recalls Gill. The U.S. Army Corps of Engineers was the contracting agent for a two billion dollar naval expansion program for Saudi Arabian port cities, part of a larger twenty billion dollar construction program that the Corps of Engineers was managing in the country. Sterling silver accompanied other Saudi orders for Steuben glass, Baccarat crystal and Limoges china.

"King Khalid enjoyed the luxuries of the western world, and owning sterling silver service was eating with the finest," reflects George Gregory, director of international sales at the time. Gregory had also been head of Reed & Barton's hotel division, and the project for the Saudis drew upon the company's experience manufacturing hotel ware. Gregory remembers *Hampton Court* and *Pointed Antique* as flatware patterns selected by the Royal Family, designed with the royal naval crest of two anchors and a rope and crossed palm leaves. Several silver services were also purchased for King Khalid's Boeing 747. As the king traveled, clean sterling was brought aboard to replace the used silverware at stops along the way, recalls Sinclair Weeks Jr.

The sterling service order from the Saudi Arabian government in 1980 is well remembered for the variety of many beautiful pieces and the challenging size of some of the items, such as lamb platters. *Left to right:* Repoussé chasing on a pitcher, a teapot, coffee server, and platter. Reed & Barton archives.

A highlight of the Saudi Arabian orders was one for ten large sterling platters, four to five feet long, which rested on a rack and were intended to carry roasted lambs. Chief Engineer Tom Kluchko had to find a press large enough to accommodate the sheet of sterling, purchased from Handy and Harman, that was sixty inches long and forty inches wide. It cost $60,000 to make each die, recalls Gill. "We made all our own tooling," says Harry Gurney who was manager of manufacturing engineering. "There was no equipment big enough to press the sheet at Reed & Barton, so we found a Rhode Island company that made aircraft parts.

Henry Gill, Vice President of Manufacturing, and President of Reed & Barton Silversmiths, helped coordinate the development of automatic methods that streamlined production. 1986. Reed & Barton archives.

The tooling trials were made with copper sheets to avoid using the costly sterling for setting up. The cradle for the tray was made of three-quarter-inch sterling rod that made a pretty hefty assembly."

When it was time to deliver the order, the armed security provided by our government was unforgettable, recalls Gurney. "As the order was taken out of the shipping room to the trucks waiting in the courtyard, the military stood guard, armed to the teeth with side arms, submachine guns, and battle gear, as a helicopter hovered overhead. It was unbelievable, like a movie."

Company records show contracts received in June 1980 which called for fifty custom-made sterling items, totaling 3,318 pieces. These were made for the Saudis during 1980–81. A partial listing includes lamb trays and racks, waiters, serving plates, punch bowls, a variety of trays, coffee and tea sets, chafing dishes, pitchers, serving spoons, and dishes. The production schedule and total lead time for delivery ranged from twenty to forty-one weeks after the receipt of the June order.

Specifications for one lamb platter included a sterling metal blank measuring 36-by-46-by-.080 inches, with a finished weight of 480.25 troy ounces for each tray. By comparison, relates Leonard, who worked on the project, the lamb platter had three times the sterling content of the largest *Francis I* waiter made by the company at 165 troy ounces. "It was a project that was out of the ordinary, slow and exacting. The body of the trays was formed outside our plant and assembled in pieces. Every one of the over 3,000 pieces of holloware had a serial number. It was an extraordinary undertaking."

In addition to sterling, stainless and silverplated holloware began to grow, requiring the expansion of plant facilities. Gill remembers when Reed & Barton silverplated flatware and holloware became part of the "New Look" at Eastern Airlines "Famous Restaurants" flights in 1965. Unfortunately, loss and pilferage of the silverware resulted in the airline's reluctantly switching to stainless flatware.

The two-day grand opening of the Sheraton-Boston at the Prudential Center on the nineteenth and twentieth of April 1965 is remembered by Gill. "Each guest received a silverplated bowl made by Reed & Barton as a souvenir. Reed & Barton was supplying silverware for the Sheraton hotels worldwide then. Reed & Barton is the oldest manufacturer of hotel silverware in the nation. For many years, substantial weight and heavy silverplating was the preference for fine dining before improved design caused a growing challenge by stainless."

Sterling flatware for the Saudi Arabian government displays royal crests. 1980. Reed & Barton archives.

In 1972 Reed & Barton learned that Israel Farber, owner and manager of the Sheffield Silver Company, an established plated holloware manufacturer located in New York City, was interested in selling. Helping Reed & Barton assess the benefits of acquiring Sheffield Silver for access to the moderate, lower priced plated market, for giftware and catalogue sales, was Charles Rodgers, the former president of the Poole Silver Company in Taunton. Experienced in design and silver production, Rodgers and Reed & Barton were well acquainted with one another. Following World War I, he left his native Austria because of the poor economy and went to England. When the ominous rise of Hitler threatened the peace of Europe in the late 1930s, Rodgers came to America, arriving with a slip of paper on which the name and address of Reed & Barton had been recommended. He worked at Reed & Barton through the war years and then became the president of the Poole Silver Company, where he learned how to make medium-grade silverware inexpensively.

Thirty years later, once again in Reed & Barton's employ, he found many similarities to the family-owned Sheffield Silver Company and supported its purchase. He supervised the initial move to Norton, Massachusetts, at the site of the former Talbot Woolen Mill, which was acquired by Reed & Barton to house both the Eureka Corporation and the Sheffield Corporation. Rodgers was appointed president and Farber, vice president and head of sales; and Reed & Barton entered a new marketing arena for plated silver.

Following World War II, Reed & Barton began to manufacture commercial stainless steel, mainly for the company's hotel line. Previously, management was opposed to using the Reed & Barton name for stainless, which was marketed instead under the name Rebacraft. In 1957 Hurley, encouraged by Hallowell, planned a marketing campaign for stainless flatware, which by the middle 1950s was facing competition from Japanese imports. Improved manufacturing techniques, such as the use of automatic polishing machines, helped to keep costs competitive; and by the end of 1969 stainless was an established part of Reed & Barton, though accounting for only 4.5 percent of total sales.

Stainless steel is an alloy made of steel that contains iron, chromium, and nickel. Chromium enhances corrosion resistance, and nickel provides luster while allowing for pattern definition and detail. The chemical alloy most often purchased by consumers is 18/8 stainless steel, which is eighteen parts chromium and eight parts nickel. This combination has proven over time to effectively combine the best attributes of tarnish free, easy-care cleaning for stainless steel flatware.

When Reed & Barton acquired the Scientific Silver Corporation in 1982, a major distributor and importer of stainless steel, it was welcoming an old friend with a long association to the company. Scientific Silver was founded in 1937 by Win Nichols and John Moody, who early on recognized the importance of stainless steel flatware for the future. Originally, the company, named Scientific Cleaning Corporation, was a service business that cleaned and polished silverware for hotels and restaurants. Nichols describes it as "a laundry service for silverware." At night the silver was taken from hotels and restaurants to be polished and cleaned and then returned the next day.

In 1941 the company was renamed the Scientific Silver Service Corporation and expanded to selling stainless flatware, initially to restaurants and hotels and then for home use. Reed & Barton manufactured the stainless steel flatware that Scientific Silver distributed to houseware departments in department stores and catalogue showrooms. During the 1950s the increase in imported flatware, first from Europe, then from the Orient, accounted for a larger share of the stainless flatware market. Initially, stainless was regarded as just a "hunk of steel," recalls Nichols, used for such casual occasions as picnics. Design and craftsmanship improved the aesthetics of stainless and with the practicality of upkeep, its popularity would only rise, predicted Nichols. The acquisition of Scientific Silver, remarks President Sinclair Weeks Jr., made Reed & Barton a larger player in the "dynamic and growing stainless steel business. This strengthens and diversifies us."

Improved designs, variety, and higher quality of product have made stainless a growing metal of choice for consumers and increased sales revenue for the company. Dollar sales from stainless flatware began to surpass those of sterling by 1997 at Reed & Barton. The same year Waterford Crystal added flatware to their crystal and china offerings through a licensed agreement with Reed & Barton. Four Waterford stainless patterns, marketed by Reed & Barton, made their debut at the New York City October 1997 Tabletop Show. Each flatware pattern was also produced with a 24-karat gold accent, reflective of the growing trend in tableware with gold accents. Since 1989 Reed & Barton has had a flatware license agreement with the Ralph Lauren Company, the largest designer label in tabletop, which has proved very successful.

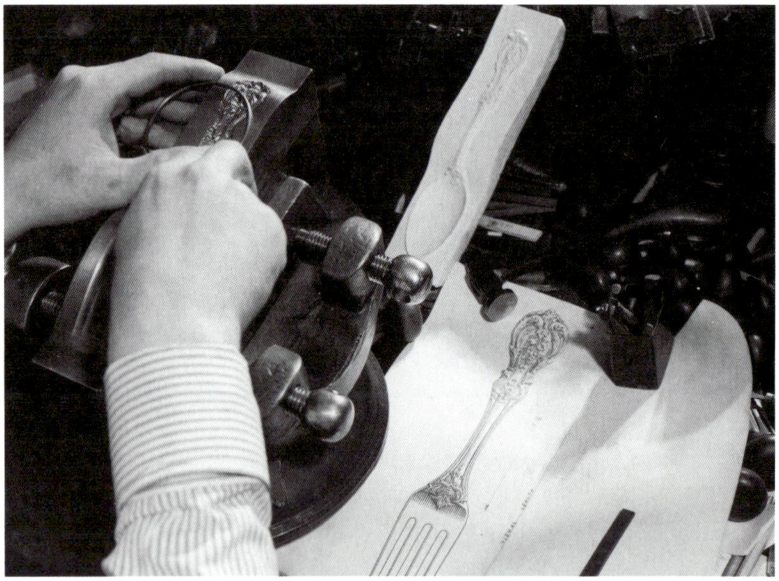

B K

Above left to right: Die preparation before stamping; fork as a blank, ready to stamp; fork stamped with flash; fork cleaned and surfaced.

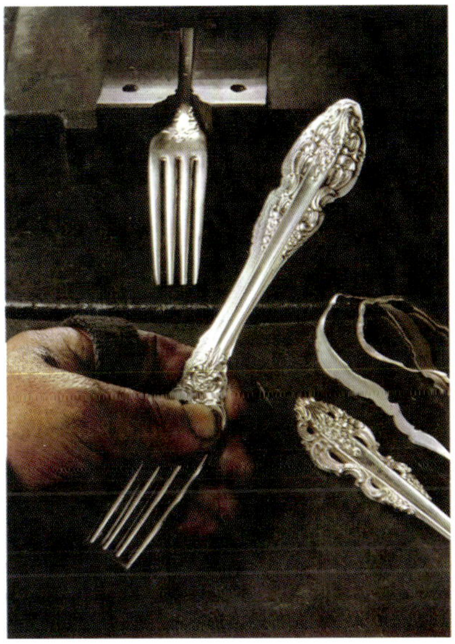

Below left to right: Billy King, die cutter. 1988.

Alfred Soares, flatware stamper. 1998.

Sue Holmes, flatware plater, using automatic machine. 1998.

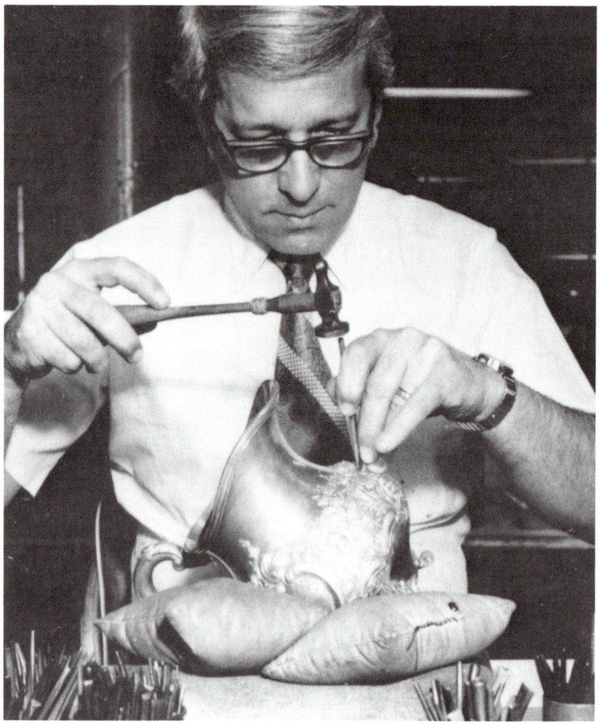

Clockwise left to right: Jim Almeida, silversmith, chasing. 1950.

Vernon Oldfield, silversmith, soldering handle on tea pot. 1976.

Mike Radevicz and Keith Franklin, silversmiths, prepare to shape the Corrigan's Cup polo trophy into sixteen matching facets. 1984.

Blanche Purcell, silversmith, hard silver soldering sterling teaware. 1998.

Mike Radevicz, silversmith, hammering sterling teaware. 1998.

Reed & Barton archives.

For a time Reed & Barton would not sell to retailers that discounted the price of sterling, a practice prevalent in New York City, but with the accompanying loss of business eventually conceded that price was a major determinant in the market. With stainless steel there proved to be a lot of competition beginning in the 1960s, explains Gill. "The finished product could be imported at a lower price than the cost of U.S. made raw material, and 80 percent of stainless steel now comes from overseas. We were making the highest quality products, but people were buying Chevies not Cadillacs. The industry really changed in the late 1970s. Stainless flatware and holloware were increasingly outsourced first to Japan, Taiwan, and Korea, then to Thailand and China, always seeking the lowest labor costs. Speculation had forced the price of sterling up in the late 1970s, and brides began to prioritize other home items ahead of sterling. The dual problems of silver costs and import competition have raised havoc with the industry."

The children of the baby boom who grew up in the late 1960s and during the 1970s married later, eschewing past traditions. "During the hippie era, big weddings were out," Robert Johnston, director of the Sterling Silversmiths Guild of America told the *New York Times* in an interview about changes in the silver industry. "People were getting married in the pasture with a guitar and no one was giving silver presents." While in the 1950s through the mid 1960s it was common for a bride to receive silverware, much of it from Reed & Barton, relates Gill, by the 1970s and 1980s wood, cookware, and household items replaced silverware.

Sinclair Weeks Jr., *right,* and Paul Sullivan, foreman of the Holloware Making Department, discuss production methods. 1980. Reed & Barton archives.

The 1960s and 1970s were decades of change and experimentation. The "let's try this, let's make that" freewheeling thinking that would have unnerved many only energized Gill, working in production management, who became vice president of production in 1971 and vice president of manufacturing in 1975. "To me it was an obvious challenge. I was let go on my own and I had more damn fun making new machinery. We developed major improvements in the entire plant utilizing new materials, methods and automated machinery, which increased productivity and reduced costs significantly. We essentially revamped the entire manufacturing process over a period of eight years."

Automated processes were introduced and high cost labor-intensive procedures reduced. "We used to have nine chasers; now we have one," explains Gill. "Labor costs are high for chasing. To make a stylized coffee service would take three days and cost $320 a day. We used to do a lot of hand spinning, then introduced automatic presses which saved a lot of time and were cheaper. The skilled work of the hand grease buffer was replaced by the automatic buffing machine

Vice President of Manufacturing Jim Butcher, *left*, with Plant Superintendent Butch Leonard. 1998. Reed & Barton archives.

which could do many more pieces per hour and resulted in a tremendous change in production costs."

Automatic machines that streamlined production were being developed throughout the factory. "We looked at every operation and found a better way to do it," says Gill. "We revamped the whole manufacturing process to get the best equipment and standards. We reduced the time it took to work on plated holloware by one-third. As workers became more productive and we were able to increase the volume of sales, more contemporary space was required. In 1958 we expanded our flatware facilities and in 1968 our holloware plant.

"Automatic buffing machines, coupled with more sophisticated tooling and higher quality materials, enabled us to eliminate a significant portion of sand polishing and hand grease buffing, with a minimal amount of touch-up required before a piece was ready for plating. Improved methods of stamping and forming, plus better materials, created a superior surface. Centrifugal casting with multiple cavity rubber molds enabled us to increase productivity significantly and virtually eliminated the making of bronze molds.

"Buffing experienced the most change in hand operations. We could go directly from the stamping operation to grease buffing, eliminating sand polishing, except on serving pieces like a gravy ladle. One or two operators could now load brass and nickel silver items on an automatic plating machine. The air drop hammer could be set on automatic. Automatic die making and stamping machines were introduced and split dies developed. The engineers achieved a real breakthrough in making blades. An automatic annealing and forming operation enabled knife blades to be made as one integrated unit. We modified machines and when necessary built them ourselves. I visited and talked to manufacturers and machinists and learned about operations from other companies. Quality was our number one objective and we achieved that. Reed & Barton was one of the last companies to outsource plated holloware in the 1990s."

Vice President of Manufacturing Jim Butcher succeeded Gill when he became president of Reed & Barton Silversmiths in 1987. The company was facing further consolidation. Reed & Barton's Houseware Division was closed in Connecticut and moved into a portion of the former holloware facility in Taunton. Fifty employees from the company's Sheffield Silver plant in Norton were also relocated there in 1991, the result of the continued decline in demand for silverplated holloware.

"Silversmiths viewed themselves as craftsmen in an industrial environment, specialists in a given area who could not be easily cross trained," explains Butcher. When the company purchased a chemical etching process that could duplicate dies, where once there were twenty-five die cutters, only four or five were needed. Weekly layoffs began. New jobs offered were frequently at less pay. A day rate replaced piecework as a more cost-effective method of payment. "While piecework offered an incentive for greater production with individual operations, it didn't result in a completed product."

Fortunately there has been a good working relationship with the union, which had been involved from the beginning with the problems of a diminishing market and the need for consolidation and economies of scale. "We worked with the union to maintain a minimum production crew in holloware for Christmas items and for some limited sterling items. We have had to learn to be flexible because the environment is continuously changing. Operations have changed from a factory that has made goods to increasingly a distributor of products for the tabletop business, where attention is on improved packaging, receiving, and shipping operations."

Reed & Barton still is the biggest company in Taunton and the most stable, says Gill. "Our presence has been felt in community fund raising, such as United Way, Morton Hospital, the banks, and among the families of the many workers we hired. At one time there were twelve hundred employees of English, French, Lithuanian, Polish, and Portuguese backgrounds. Workers could trust us." For many years Gill represented the company with the union and was well respected by workers for his fairness in negotiations.

During his thirty-seven-year career, Gill was one of the Reed & Barton executives "on loan" to the community. Taunton has been the fortunate beneficiary of the interest shown "from the silver plant on the banks of the Mill River," wrote the *Taunton Daily Gazette,* in appreciation at Gill's retirement in 1990. "Reed & Barton has been more than Taunton's 'granddaddy' industry, more than a place to work, or a source of luxurious silver products. It has been, at least for the last forty years, as much a part of Taunton as any individual who has owned a home here or rented one."

In 1900 when Dwight F. Davis, the first captain of the Davis Cup team, commissioned Shreve, Crump & Low to create a trophy for the first international tennis tournament of the United States Lawn Tennis Association, an esteemed world team competition began. The 1999 Davis Cup tournament closes the century where it began at the Longwood Cricket Club in Chestnut Hill, Massachusetts; and Shreve, Crump and Low was once again called upon, this time to refurbish the Davis Cup, removing its accumulated dents and blemishes. It was a job Shreve's gave to Reed & Barton, along with the request to design and construct a new base for the sterling trophy. Director of Design Clark Lofgren's three-tiered base, crafted of solid Honduras mahogany, provides space to engrave another forty-five years of Davis Cup winners.

Ready for the competition, Reed & Barton's Davis Cup team *from left to right:* Raymond Gwozdz, new product coordinator; Michael Radevicz, silversmith; Clark Lofgren, director of design; and Catherine Barrett-Cornwall, product development manager. 1998. Reed & Barton archives.

THE SYNERGY between Reed & Barton silver and Eureka's wooden chests was a natural, and a working association began long before the acquisition of the Eureka Manufacturing Company as a subsidiary in 1966. Forty years earlier when Sinclair Weeks Sr. was president of Reed & Barton, the decision was made to sell the bag and roll department and related sewing equipment to Ernest Gebelein's newly founded Eureka company in 1926. The work continued to be done for many years at a leased Reed & Barton factory building.

When brother Arthur Gebelein joined the company in 1934, the product line broadened to include silverware chests, with Oneida as their biggest customer. "For a time, prior to Reed & Barton's acquisition, Eureka shipped as much as a railroad car of chests a week to Oneida," relates Charles Terry, Reed & Barton treasurer and former president of Eureka. "These chests were largely designed by Gebelein to match the flatware patterns they were to hold, and at this time nearly all the Oneida flatware was silverplate instead of sterling or stainless."

But the rise of stainless steel flatware sharply reduced the demand for silver chests, and Oneida ceased purchasing entirely. A strike closed the chest division in 1958 and Gebelein reopened a few months later as the Wood Specialties Company. "He made many of the machines used in production or adapted them for specific uses," says Terry. A mechanically inventive individual, Arthur Gebelein was oriented to technique and design, though not to sales and production. By 1965 the Gebelein brothers were ready to sell and, with Reed & Barton as one of their three principal customers along with Gorham and Towle, approached President Roger Hallowell. If Reed & Barton were to acquire Eureka, a competent management team was needed to run the company.

Jewelry chests crafted at Eureka Manufacturing Company quickly became best sellers for Reed & Barton. 1998. Reed & Barton archives.

The acquisition of Eureka ensured a source of quality chests, and Reed & Barton's sales force could sell the chests and non-tarnish Pacific Silvercloth, a cloth that had silver nitrate impregnated in it, through their regular lines of distribution. The terms of the purchase and sale agreement signed on 7 February 1966 permitted Arthur Gebelein to be president for five years. His propensity to handle all production problems in the shop, however, diverted his attention from broader administrative matters. "At the time there was no piecework incentive. Most of the work force made minimum wage and as a result there was high absenteeism and low productivity," says Terry. "The stitching department that made bags for the storing of silver products did have an incentive system and as a result had a more stable work force."

Charles P. Terry, President of Eureka Manufacturing Company from 1974 to 1991, helped to integrate an incentive system which provided the basis for a stable work force. In 1991 Terry became Senior Vice President of Finance and Treasurer, Reed & Barton. 1998. Reed & Barton archives.

Harry Burbank, retired sales manager for Eureka, started his long career at the company in 1940 and, except for World War II service time, remained through 1981, long enough to see silver reach fifty dollars an ounce. Burbank is a veteran of the road, remembering thirteen-week assignments at a time away from home. When it got too lonesome, he would hop a flight back for the weekend. "It always took about three days to get over the long faces of my wife and kids when I left."

Eureka chests were a top quality product to sell, and before the Reed & Barton days low inventory was the main problem facing sales staff. "We tried to limit our sales to the carriage trade and better department stores, one in each city." Burbank remembers the Franklin Mint as a very demanding customer. "Because we shipped through the mail, they would put our products through the 'drop test' to see if they would pass without breaking. Eureka manufactured chests for ingots, coins, medallions, and birds, flags, automobiles, and governors of the state, all of which they heavily advertised. They promoted a superior product with a high price."

When sterling silver was a big seller, chests were mainly used for silverware storage, but with the growth of stainless steel, jewelry boxes became the larger revenue producer. Specialty uses followed, such as cases manufactured for Parker pens in the early 1980s with a mariners' theme using brass from the portholes of the *QE II;* there were boxes made for games, as well as keepsake boxes for jewelry from the deceased made for casket companies. Eureka became the largest user of Pacific cloth for bags and rolls and for lining better chests. Though silver nitrate Pacific cloth would last a lifetime, the less expensive Hagerty Silversmiths' Cloth impregnated with zinc nitrate became a good seller for the company. The bag and roll business was strong when sterling was widely used and silver needed protection, explains Burbank, while putting the store's name on the cloth bag added to its marketing appeal.

Reed & Barton's investment in Eureka as a totally owned subsidiary was $300,000. Charles Terry was hired in September 1966 to improve the cost and general accounting at both the Webster Company, a subsidiary silver company that was sold two years later, and Eureka. An incentive program was developed in 1968 that remains in effect today, says Terry. "It enables the individual worker to set the rate of production within specified guidelines, giving the employee some control over his or her rate of pay and ultimately increasing overall production."

Donald F. Morrison, Senior Vice President of Administration and Treasurer, began his career at Eureka in 1962 and continues to be an integral part of the company's success. 1998. Reed & Barton archives.

There was little progress at the company until the early 1970s when Eureka started making chests for the Franklin Mint's "Collectors' Coins," "which required a more efficient and disciplined operation," says Terry who became president in 1974, when the growing company moved to Norton. Eureka occupied a portion of the former Talbot Wool Company building, purchased by Reed & Barton a few years earlier to house the Sheffield Silver Company. "The work for the Franklin Mint gave Eureka the volume it needed to afford production improvements, the confidence that they had a viable business, and a steady stream of orders for a wide range of chest sizes and designs to accommodate their full range of collectibles," says Terry. "As new employees were hired, the work force became more and more first generation Portuguese who were offered incentives to bring friends and relatives to Eureka. A conscientious and hard working group, they made the piecework incentive system succeed both for themselves and the company. Though they comprise over 60 percent of the work force today, the strength of the other employees should not be overlooked."

President Sinclair Weeks Jr. had hired the right man with Terry to lead the turnaround. Don Morrison, senior vice president of administration and treasurer at Eureka, began his career in the shipping room in 1962, until Terry discovered his accounting degree. He credits Terry's interest and style in promoting good labor relations. "You could talk to Chuck about anything. Having the door open was the key to stabilizing the workforce," while Terry depended on Morrison's "tireless energy."

Economies of production were realized when Eureka began purchasing dimensioned wooden blanks in the late 1970s, rather than producing their own. "A tremendous time saver with no waste," says Morrison. Other time saving

Above, The Concorde Humidor. All of the company's humidors feature a humidification system and hygrometer. Humidors store and age cigars at an ideal level of humidity to enhance their flavor. 1996. Reed & Barton archives.

Silverware chests, such as the Provincial model, ideally complement Reed & Barton flatware. Each chest is handcrafted from American hardwood, receives a hand-rubbed finish, and is fitted and lined with tarnish-preventive cloth. 1996. Reed & Barton archives.

Above, Athena, an impressive three-drawer jewelry chest, provides storage for an extensive collection of jewelry. 1996. Reed & Barton archives.

Right, The Grand Chippendale Table Chest is the largest and most impressive of Eureka's silver storage chests. With a capacity of up to 230 pieces of flatware, it is fully lined with tarnish-preventive cloth. 1997. Reed & Barton archives.

Chris A. Costa, Vice President of Manufacturing, has integrated new technology into the traditional manufacturing environment. 1998. Reed & Barton archives.

machinery, he explains, such as the automatic shaper and sander, not only cut costs, but also more importantly reduced injuries because the hands of workers were no longer near the blades. Machinery that minimizes hand operations is continuously researched.

By 1985 Eureka had exceeded four million dollars in sales, relates Terry, with the retail business through the Reed & Barton sales force driving the company. "An extensive line of chests for silverware and jewelry was in place and occasionally the company contracted to produce custom boxes, such as Colt 45 pistol boxes and collectible boxes for the Danbury Mint."

The appointment of Chris Costa in 1987 as plant manager resulted in a vigorous program to modernize and upgrade machinery. He established a purchased parts program that eliminated many dangerous and laborious hand tasks in woodworking, organized a more efficient factory layout, and improved personnel supervision that resulted in increased productivity. Today as vice president of manufacturing, Costa continues to assess equipment upgrades for production, and safety remains a high priority at Eureka. "These priorities have placed Eureka at the top of the woodworking industry," says Costa.

In 1991 Terry was appointed senior vice president of finance and treasurer of Reed & Barton; and George Gregory, who had been the president of Sheffield Silver prior to its absorption at Reed & Barton, became president of Eureka for two years before he retired in 1993. Terry continued in an advisory role until the appointment of David McLoughlin as president in 1995. The turnaround and profitability of Eureka has been a success story, explains Terry. "Since 1975 Eureka has always earned a profit for Reed & Barton. With only a relatively small amount of capital invested in Eureka, the return on assets has been good, providing cash and earnings for Reed & Barton when times were tough. The company is now capitalizing on opportunity, seizing the moment with the popularity of cigars to manufacture humidors."

The United States State Department orders about twenty-five flatware chests a year for their embassies, explains Morrison. "The wood is Appalachian poplar, fast growing and sturdy, that comes from Pennsylvania, North Carolina, and Maryland. Presidents Ronald Reagan and George Bush have Reed & Barton flatware chests. In November 1995 we began making humidors."

With the manufacturing of humidors, Reed & Barton at the Eureka plant not only entered a new market for their wooden chests, but a new avenue of mar-

David P. McLoughlin, President of Eureka Manufacturing Company, energetically pursues additional markets and uses for wooden chests. 1998. Reed & Barton archives.

keting. At the J. C. Newman Cigar Company's centennial celebration in September 1995, the Newmans introduced Diamond Crown humidors developed in partnership with Reed & Barton, which have become the nation's best-selling humidor collection.

Eureka has filled the rising need for humidors to become the largest manufacturer nationally. While cigarette smokers are increasingly unwelcome in public places, cigar smokers are viewed as upscale. Diamond Crown cigars and Diamond Crown humidors are marketed with the Reed & Barton name for recognition and simplification, explains President David McLoughlin.

The expanded use of wooden chests from silverware and jewelry to high-grade packaging that enhances other products is energetically promoted by McLoughlin. A recent project, for example, involved the production of 7,000 wooden cases for a limited edition of Sheaffer pens. "We are taking wooden chests to new markets."

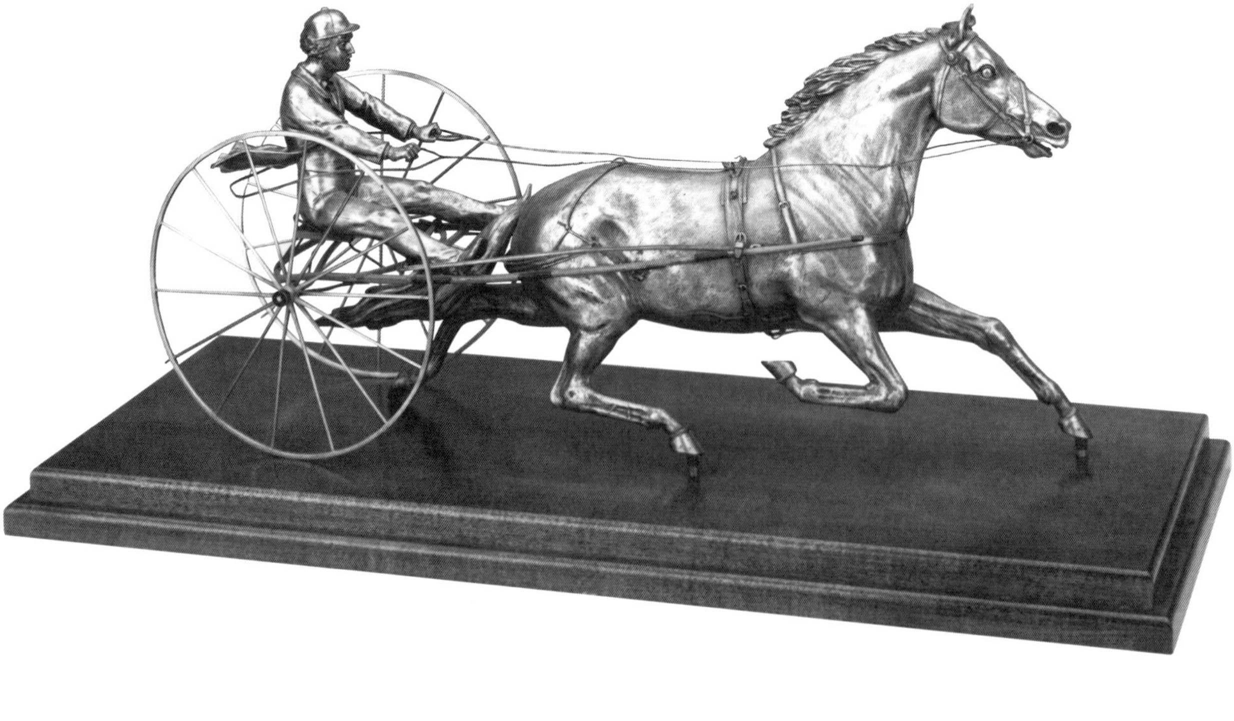

AN INDUSTRY OF CHANGE

THE SILVER industry is a tabletop industry today, sharing its berth with china and crystal. A silver company must have its pulse on a diversified product market, reflects President Al Krebel, who has experienced the transitions in the industry through the breadth of his own career that began in 1961.

Most of Krebel's career has been with the large silver manufacturing companies, beginning as a salesman for Wallace and successively becoming the vice president of sales and marketing for Gorham and president of International Silver. He has seen the major silver companies lose their individual identities and become part of large conglomerates. "International Silver Company, Wallace Silversmiths, and Towle Silversmiths are divisions of Syratech Corporation, owned by Thomas H. Lee Company, a Boston leveraged-buyout firm. Textron acquired the Gorham Company in 1968 and then sold it to Dansk. Brown-Forman Corporation acquired Dansk and Gorham and consolidated both with their Lenox consumer durable division. Lenox also owns Kirk Stieff. Oneida, in Oneida, New York, is a NYSE traded company. Only Lunt Silversmiths remains a privately held silver company similar to Reed & Barton."

Henry Reed's nineteenth-century horse and sulky with rider moves into the twenty-first century. A timeless display of Reed's wish to have one or more masterpieces in production at the factory at all times. Circa 1875. Reed & Barton archives.

Reed & Barton retains its independent identity under the Weeks family ownership. When Sinclair Weeks Jr. announced his intent to retire as president in 1987 and become chairman of the board, Reed & Barton looked outside the company to fill the position. Krebel was president of Farberware when a search firm approached him. "In a small industry where people know one another, Reed & Barton had the highest reputation," says Krebel. "The brand name, the history of the company and knowing that Sinny was going to be Chairman of the Board, all influenced my decision. I had met Sinny through the years and knew how well he was regarded. There was incredible loyalty by retailers to the company and good strength and capability within a range of departments."

By bringing a fresh approach, Krebel could more readily evaluate the areas of growth and restructure or sell other product lines and divisions. "Jewelry was not a strategic fit, while Eureka's chests were, so the latter business was aggressively developed and investments were made to increase product assortment and manufacturing capacity. Holloware demand was experiencing a continuous decline so the Sheffield Company was consolidated into the Reed & Barton factory. Later as demand continued to decline, the Reed & Barton holloware facility was aggressively downsized. The competitive market for collectibles and the overexposure of direct response marketing resulted in the decision to exit that business."

President Al Krebel. "By quickly reacting to the needs of the marketplace, Reed & Barton is a survivor in the silver industry." 1998. Reed & Barton archives.

Krebel charted a new course that has successfully broadened Reed & Barton's outreach. This includes the distribution rights for Belleek china and Galway crystal from Ireland; acquiring the crystal company of Miller Rogaska; licensing agreements for the manufacture of Ralph Lauren flatware and giftware and for Waterford flatware; marketing through televised home shopping; and American Express direct mail efforts.

There were skills and talents at the company for Krebel to capitalize on. "Reed & Barton is strong in sales and marketing, and we have good in-house product development. The company produces or sources 135 flatware patterns in various metals and knows how to go to market with a product."

The marketplace has changed dramatically, however, in the last decade, relates Krebel. "Getting our product in front of the customer is the biggest challenge. So few retailers have an adequate display area or staff willing to care for silver. Stainless steel, made in the Orient, is strongest in the department stores, while sterling and silverplate are featured in independent stores. A dozen Reed & Barton factory outlet stores have been introduced throughout the nation. It is a great way for the company and buying public to have direct contact and a lot of inventory moves through this channel.

"The number of upscale independent stores that traditionally featured silver has declined. Many department stores are phasing out holloware and do not have staff knowledgeable about silver, while far fewer restaurants feature plated flatware. Stainless has therefore become a larger volume of Reed & Barton's business and recently has passed sterling in sales dollars. Often the consumer doesn't realize the time and money that goes into better quality silver crafting and is more influenced by price. By quickly reacting to the needs of the marketplace, Reed & Barton is a survivor in the silver industry. Reaching the milestone of our 175th birthday, the company is profitable, healthy, and growing."

Sinclair Weeks Jr. "A company, like a country, reflects the accumulation of past events, and many of the shaping forces have roots in prior generations." 1983. Reed & Barton archives.

Reflecting on Reed & Barton's long history, Chairman Sinclair Weeks Jr. observes that over the past one hundred seventy-five years, there have been only seven company presidents while the nation and silver industry have experienced major transformations. "It has been correctly stated that 'the only thing in life you can be sure of is change,' and this is particularly true of an organization so closely tied to the tastes and lifestyle of the people of this rapidly growing and prosperous country of ours. Each of these seven men learned to live with change and their unique contributions have established, grown and perpetuated the company over a period of years only four decades less than the entire history of the United States republic itself.

"Henry Reed with his partner Charles Barton laid the foundation, established the culture, and developed the company over an extraordinary personal business career of seventy-three years from 1828 to 1901. Reed's creativity in the development of product and his concern for maintaining the highest standards of quality established a reputation for Reed & Barton silverware which is unequalled. Through the vicissitudes of war and economic calamity, the company grew with the support of a loyal customer base. Reed came from Taunton and what the business gave to the community was returned a hundred-fold in the loyalty and support of its citizens and institutions. And so with this combination of good human relations in the plant, fine product quality, loyal customers, and a supportive community, Henry Reed established the heritage that continues to this day.

"William B. H. Dowse, my maternal grandfather, who followed Reed, was an able patent lawyer who consolidated financial control and brought exceptional design talent to the company, establishing a retail presence in New York City during that era. My father, Sinclair Weeks, faced the enormous challenge of bringing the company through the Great Depression of the 1930s. Those were the days when for an employee to get a new pencil he or she had to turn in the stub of the old!

"My brother-in-law Roger H. Hallowell, formerly a teacher and decorated PT boat skipper in World War II, reestablished and greatly enhanced the company's

Reed & Barton is the sole U.S. distributor of Belleek Parian china from Belleek, Ireland. Reed & Barton archives.

Right, Hand-painted shamrock grouping includes the Kylemore Vase and Planter, and Leitrim Vase. 1992.

Enchanted Garden Collection features pansies and combines relief and transfer design. 1998.

Belleek Claddagh Collection combines bisque and glaze with detailed relief work. 1992.

Below left, Bloomfield Commemorative Vase for the 140th anniversary of Belleek, 1997. At the end of the year, the mold for the vase was destroyed, enhancing the collectibility of the piece.

Below right, Beauty Rose hand-woven, hand-painted baskets. 1996.

The production of crystal in Rogaska, Slovenia, began in 1860. The factory there has grown to become the world's largest producer of handmade crystal. The Miller Rogaska company, formed in 1984 to import and distribute full lead crystal from the Rogaska factory, was acquired by Reed & Barton in 1997. Angie Miller, the daughter of founder John Miller, continues as president. Reed & Barton archives.

Opposite page and right, Richmond Giftware, one of the first collections offered by Miller Rogaska, remains a favorite today.

Opposite page, below, Soho Barware is one of the best sellers in the Miller Rogaska product line and is the most registered barware pattern at Bloomingdale stores.

Below, Soho Square Twist Vase, one of the first Miller Rogaska items to be produced in an "out of round" format.

Below right, Triangle Collection, a highly stylized design enhanced by the clarity and quality of the crystal.

Reed & Barton Board of Directors:
Left to right:
Front row: William D. Weeks, Charles P. Terry, Albert D. Krebel, Sinclair Weeks Jr., John K. Spring, Nelson S. Gifford, John W. Weeks Jr. *Rear:* Timothy T. More, William H. Dykstra, Ernest E. Siegfreidt Jr., Alvin J. Silk, Carol Ann Hayes, Russell D. Wright. (John W. Weeks is not in photo). April 1998. Reed & Barton archives.

interest and development of new silverware product. In the 1950s and 1960s Reed & Barton became known for exciting new sterling flatware patterns which so well reflected the taste of the women of America. Color Glaze, Damascene, and the beginning products of stainless steel also met with growing customer acceptance and demonstrated the creative technical and design energies of the company.

"My own administration followed and was also a period of challenge and change. Continuing to recognize that the future growth of fine sterling and plated ware would be limited by the change of lifestyles and distribution channels, companies such as Scientific Silver Service and the Sheffield Silver Company were acquired. Eureka Manufacturing Company was reorganized and given new management following the acquisition of the Norton, Massachusetts, property. The Fiscal year of 1980 included the attempted 'silver corner' by the

Hunt Brothers and was certainly the most chaotic year in the history of the company. Silver sales to the Kingdom of Saudi Arabia was an experience never likely to be repeated; the period of deep discounting which prompted litigation with our competitors to stop this practice (which we eventually won); and the adoption of Sub-Chapter S. status for Reed & Barton were highlights of a continuing period of activity and change.

"In 1987 Albert D. Krebel, with deep, varied, and successful experience in our industry, became President and set about further changes and redirecting the business. Early in the 1990s when the banks were under great pressure from the regulators and accordingly put similar pressure on their own customers, Krebel and Senior Vice President of Finance Bill Dykstra were under constant pressure to decrease debt, lower inventories, and increase cash flow. They accomplished the desired results through exceptional leadership, great energy, and an accurate focus on the problems.

"Marketing has become even more dominant as certain manufactured lines have been discontinued. The distribution of Belleek porcelain and Galway Crystal, the expansion of Factory outlet stores throughout the country, the acquisition in 1996 of the Miller Rogaska Company for crystal, licensing agreements with Ralph Lauren and Waterford, and direct mail sales promotion through American Express–all underlie the continued growth, diversity, and prosperity of Reed & Barton.

"And so the view from active retirement continues to be interesting and exciting. What comes into clearer focus when one is removed from the daily management problems can be summarized. A company, like a country, reflects the accumulation of past events, and many of the shaping forces have roots in prior generations. How do you perpetuate the enduring character of an organization? What are the essential and lasting beliefs, the timeless guiding principles, and the company's basic reasons for being? It is better to understand who you are than where you are going, for the road, the path ahead, will certainly change.

"Finally, leadership and good human relations have much in common. In the years to come there will be changes in life styles, work environments, and work habits as well as the kind of work to be done. With these changes, the 'glue' which holds the organization together may well become increasingly ideological, less personal and physical. People have a fundamental need to belong to something they can be proud of, for guiding values and a sense of purpose that gives meaning to life and work."

Bibliography Index

BIBLIOGRAPHY

General Reference

Bumiller, Elisabeth. "A Touch of Glass for Saudi Navy." *Washington Post,* as printed in the *Detroit News,* 11 March 1980.

Bury, Robert. "Leonard, Reed & Barton, et al." *The Pewter Collectors Club of America Bulletin* 11, no. 8 (winter 1997).

Cunningham, John B. *The Story of Belleek.* Belleek, N. Ireland: St. Davog's Press, 1992.

Dolan, Maryanne. *American Sterling Silver Flatware: A Collector's Identification and Value Guide.* Florence, Ala.: Books Americana, 1993.

Edwards, Maxine T. *Mermaids and Saguaros: The USS Arizona Silver.* Phoenix: Arizona State Capitol Museum, Museum Division of the Arizona Department of Library, Archives and Public Records, 1994.

Fay, Stephen. *Beyond Greed.* New York: Viking Press, 1982.

Gibb, George Sweet. *The Whitesmiths of Taunton.* Cambridge: Harvard University Press, 1943.

Harrop, Froma. "The Fine-Dining Market Isn't Enough." *New York Times,* 7 January 1990.

—. "Add-ons Ease the Pain of Shrinking Silver Sales." *New York Times,* 7 January 1990.

King, Andrew C. Jr., ed. *Taunton Celebration of the Massachusetts Bay Tercentenary, 1630–1930.* Taunton, Mass.: Taunton Tercentenary Committee, 1930.

Quinn, Jane Bryant. "High Prices Tarnish Sterling Silver Sales." *Boston Globe,* 12 May 1980.

"Reed & Barton Silversmiths: Fine Craftmanship for 164 Years." *Business Digest* (November 1988): 2–9.

"The Reed & Barton Era." *Taunton Daily Gazette,* 26 February 1990.

"Silverware Prices Following Decline of Quotes for Silver." *Wall Street Journal,* 1 October 1981.

Sniffin, Philip L. *A Century of Silversmithing.* Taunton: Reed & Barton, 1924.

"Sterling Out of Reach for Many Brides." *Christian Science Monitor,* 21 July 1979.

"A Way with Words." *Taunton Daily Gazette,* 28 March 1994.

Weeks, Sinclair Jr. Oral history by author, tape recording and transcript, 7 November 1996. Town of Concord, Concord Free Public Library, Concord, Mass.

Reed & Barton Company Collection

Adams, E. D. to Reed & Barton. 23 April 1906. San Francisco, Cal.

Frees, Russell. "Testing Tradition: Reed & Barton, 1924–1980." Typescript, 1983.

Martin, Joseph. "Reminiscences of the Old Guard." Private memoir, December 1940.

New York Times, 8 November 1981. [Advertisement by Reed & Barton].

Reed & Barton. *Marching Together.* [World War II commemorative]. Taunton: Reed & Barton, 1947.

——. *The Silver Lining.* [The newsletter of Reed & Barton]. 1943–1995.

[Reed & Barton]. *A Selection of Photographs: Presentation Ceremonies of the Army-Navy Production Award to the Men and Women of Reed & Barton, November 19, 1943.* Taunton, Mass: Privately printed, 1943.

——. *The Silver Lining: One Hundred Twenty-Fifth Anniversary.* Taunton: Reed & Barton, 1949.

——. *The Silver Lining: One Hundred Fiftieth Anniversary.* Taunton: Reed & Barton, 1974.

"The Manufacturer of Silver Plated Ware." *Scientific American* 41, no. 19 (8 November 1879).

United States Patent and Trademark Office. Trademark for Sterling Silver-Ware. 29 July 1890.

——. Trademark, Principal Register, *The Classic American Silver.* 12 May 1981.

Weeks, Sinclair. Diary, 1968–1970.

Weeks, Sinclair Jr. Private file on diversification and industry discounting, January 1984.

Movie and Video Recordings

Hands Special. 50 min. Belleek Potteries, 1987. Videocassette.

How to Be a Successful Hostess. 28 min. Kenneth Richter Productions, 1958. Film.

Reed & Barton Olympic Medals. [Televised newscasts]. 18 min. Reed & Barton, 1996. Videocassette.

The Romance of Silver Design. 27 min. Kenneth Richter Productions, 1953. Film.

INDEX

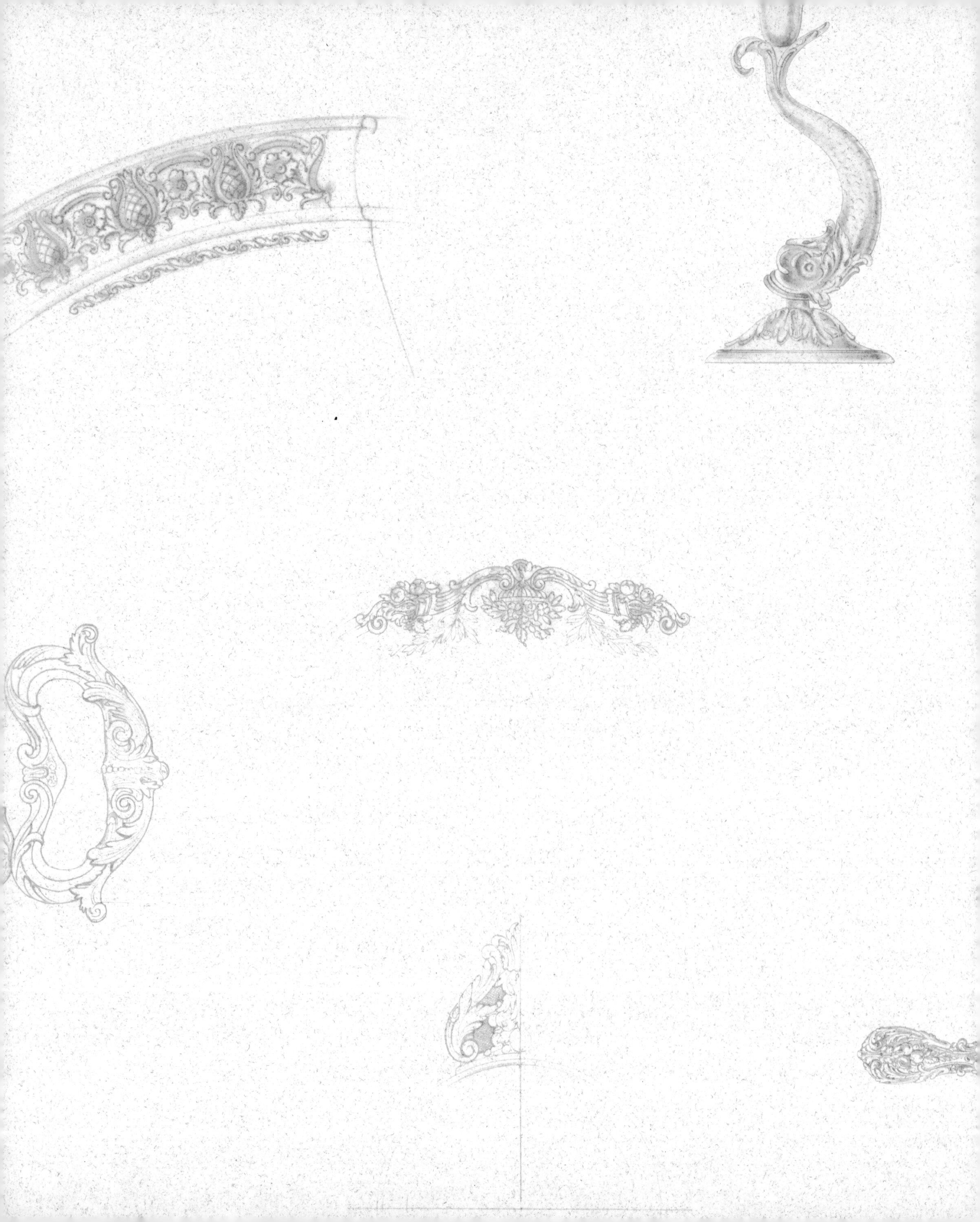